PRASE FOR *CHOOSING REAL*

"I was so inspired by Bekah's words on embracing the everyday, living fully with all of our senses, and celebrating the life right in front of us. *Choosing REAL* will motivate you to look for the beauty in the middle of the unplanned and unexpected."

—Crystal Paine, Founder of MoneySavingMom.com,
New York Times bestselling author of *Say Goodbye to Survival Mode*

"*Choosing REAL* is a fresh breath of air. The pages bring God to life; the stories inspire faithfulness; and the transparency makes the warmth of Christ's love come alive. No doubt this book will leave you feeling lighter, stronger, and a whole lot more connected to God."

—Kelly Balarie, Author of *Fear Fighting* (Baker Books),
Speaker, and Blogger at www.purposefulfaith.com

"In *Choosing REAL* Bekah has a distinct talent for a lighthearted and down-home approach that makes you feel like you're sitting on her denim couch, listening to her share her heart. I found myself encouraged to stop, appreciate the magic in the moment, and cherish the microscopic details we live in every day. She has a way of zooming into life while zooming out in perspective, encouraging us to consider what's truly important in life and realizing the molehills that feel like mountains shall pass. . .and just perhaps, there's a lesson in those molehills. When life boils down, there are a few simple key ingredients—God and people, and that's about it. Bekah's book inspires me to live in a way that has less fear and more love, because that's how God would want it, if we could just get out of our own way and 'let go and let God!'"

—Allyson Magda, Photographer of Mark and Priscilla Zuckerberg, The Hearst Family, featured on the cover of *People*, and in *Forbes*, *NY Times*, *Martha Stewart Weddings*, *World's Best Wedding Photographers*, founder of AllysonMagda.com

"Following her late father's advice to 'enjoy the journey,' Bekah Pogue invites readers to do just that. Pogue welcomes readers into all folds of her life and emphasizes what a gift it is to choose an identity built on what is real versus comparison and fantasy. Readers will find her stories refreshing in a culture that bids us to find our worth in always being picture perfect. Instead, Pogue offers anecdotes of hope amidst life's transitions and hard times. Her stories of finding God in seasons of loneliness and the ordinary moments of every day will touch readers like me who felt like I was sitting at Pogue's table with her as I read, eating a brownie and sharing our souls."

—Kristin Ritzau, Spiritual Director and Author of
A Beautiful Mess: A Perfectionist's Journey through Self-Care

"In *Choosing REAL*, Bekah Pogue artistically does just that. She chooses a journey of relentless authenticity and then invites her readers to do the same. Inspired by grief, Pogue intimately offers a front-seat view of the moments in life that are less than perfect and delicately describes how these are often the very moments in which God is perfecting Himself in us. This book is both vulnerable and inspiring, and readers will find practical application on every page to say 'YES' to the journey of life in Christ."

—Dr. Michelle Anthony, Wife, Mom, Speaker, and Author of
Spiritual Parenting, Becoming a Spiritually Healthy Family,
and *The Big God Story*

"Bekah is an enthusiastic, joyful person who projects her passion and faith on every page of *Choosing REAL*. The voice of her writing bursts with hope as she describes the challenges and complexities of managing life as a young mother. She brings comfort and spiritual inspiration to others who seek guidance on finding their own gifts and balance in our world today."

–Richard E. Felix, PhD, Author of *The School of Dying Graces*

Choosing
REAL

AN INVITATION TO CELEBRATE
WHEN LIFE DOESN'T GO AS PLANNED

Bekah Jane Pogue

DEDICATIONS

To my Father. Thank You for making Yourself Real.

To my dad, the heartbeat of this book is because of you.
Your loss was the catalyst to truly enjoying the journey. I
miss you every.single.day and can't wait to share a cheese-
burger with you in eternity. Thank you for your words on
earth and when you visit my dreams.

To my incredible hubby, Bry. There is no one I'd rather
adventure, eat, and laugh through life with than you—my
best friend and partner in crime. I absolutely adore you.

To my boys, Tanner and Ty. May you always experience
how real God is in Pokémon and playing and desserts. I am
forever a learner and fan of you both. Now run, 'cuz I hear
the "Smooching Bell" ringing.

ACKNOWLEDGMENTS

Reader friends. Thank YOU. For trusting me with your time and heart. You are the other half of this beautiful writer/reader relationship and it's your face I picture when I'm sitting at my computer—messy hair, pj's, and all. I'm honored to join you wherever you are today. Consider yourself hugged.

L'il Mom, I value *you*, your editor's eyes, intentional feedback, and unconditional cheering. Thank you. Love.you.BIG!

Mom and Dad, Uncle Paul and Aunt Kathy, and family—your support means the world. Thanks for believing in my dreams and helping make the steps toward this project possible.

To those in my "nest" and the beautiful souls whose stories are shared on these pages, *you* are my people and I couldn't have created this book without you. Thank you for putting up with my verbal processing, offering insight, praying with *and* for me, being truth-speakers, and sharing your valued perspective. Your friendship is the greatest gift. Lindsay, Stacie, Cathy, Karen, Ber, Netti, Heather, Mandy, Em and Galel, Donna, Beth and Dave, Brittany and Garrett, Drew and Jen, "Auntie" Pam, Jess, Ingrid, Jenna, Kira, Megs, Jamie, Jill, Jules, Tay, Megan, Lynette, Marlyn, Cathie, Christine, Kristy, Mana, and L'il Mom.

Blythe, what began as connecting over carrot cake led to finding an incredible agent in you, but mostly, a dear friend. You are one-of-a-kind and my life is richer with you in it. All.*is*.well.

To the fabulous Barbour team, what a joy you are to work, dream, create, and bring this book to life with. Thank you for your intentionality, personal care, and belief in this message.

And to all my dreamer sisters who have a book that needs to burst out of you, I'm cheering you on. Go for it!

CONTENTS

FOREWORD

*P*artying is hard. I mean, you can party hard, but also, the partying itself is hard to pull off. After moving to Georgia several years ago, I scoured and scrubbed my new house to get ready for a baby shower I was hosting with even newer friends. We didn't have pictures on the walls yet, and I wrapped an empty frame with wrapping paper and leaned it on the mantel over the fireplace like an extra gift for the mom-to-be to try to hide the fact that my house wasn't all put together.

I arranged the food and made coffee and pulled out all my nicest china for place settings. I didn't have enough chairs, so I resorted to a piano bench and some squishy blobby thing from the baby's playroom that leaned when I sank into it.

Putting the dogs and the baby and the husband away, I hid all indications that anyone else even lived in this home. I was entertaining guests, and they were not party approved.

My soiree was lovely, the food was delicious, and after everyone had left and I took stock of what remained, I looked down to realize I'd forgotten the dog bowls. If you have a pet, you can picture in your mind what I mean by dog bowls.

These weren't some cutesy, shiny bowls like in a commercial for Fancy Feast. These bowls had gone through daily exposure to the inside of my dogs' mouths and all they had to offer and lived to tell the tale. Told it loudly. These bowls were caked with mealy grime and covered in hair. At the base of the bowls, a brown sludge had formed, effectively sealing the bowls to the tray below with viscous goo.

And they had been there the whole time, lying guiltily on the floor at the head of the table, right by the air conditioner, which wafted the dog food smell through the air around it. Full body shudder.

Sometimes real life smells like dog bowls. Three dogs and three kids later, I am learning to *choose real*. To let people peek into my real life, filled with messy dog bowls, messy bathrooms. . .and messy faith. I don't need to hide my honest wonderings with God any more than I need to hide the dirty dog bowls from my guests.

In fact, I get to relax and be the guest of an authentic Lord who wants to meet with me. I think that's why I love Bekah's book, *Choosing Real*. It extends an invitation to experience God's real presence in our daily lives, even when those lives might not be going the way we thought they would. We don't need to clean ourselves up or hide. This book gave me permission to rest.

Bekah writes that God enjoys us, and I fully enjoyed following her through the pages of this book. She's the wise friend you want to remind you that this life is for relationship and God really likes you. We get to experience Him with all of our senses, awakened to His love all around us.

When you read this book, you just know that Bekah throws a good party. You can tell. These pages are infused with hospitality, like she's decorated the room, baked the cake, and pulled up a seat for you. And the theme? Come as you are.

—Melanie Dale, author of *It's Not Fair: Learning to Love the Life You Didn't Choose* and *Women are Scary: The Totally Awkward Adventure of Finding Mom Friends,* and blogger at Unexpected.org

INTRODUCTION

Let the attitude of your life be a continual willingness to "go out" in dependence upon God, and your life will have a sacred and inexpressible charm about it that is very satisfying to Jesus. You must learn to "go out" through your convictions, creeds, or experiences until you come to the point in your faith where there is nothing between yourself and God.

—Oswald Chambers

*J*t was weeks after my dad's sudden stroke and death that I gave up the fight. The fight that had loomed over me most of my life, the one taunting me to try harder, be peppier, keep smiling, keep giving, keep *controlling*.

Do. Do. Do.

Go. Encourage. Perform.

At a point where I finally had nothing to give anyone, I reached out, and there He was. When I opened my eyes to the awareness that faith is not something I have to muster up or reach on tiptoes to grasp, but accept as God continually pursues, it was *here* my faith came alive.

Not that it wasn't real before. It's just that I expected faith in grand doses. Epic moments. *Can someone please tell me how I can know God to be real in the middle of moves, job changes, mommy meltdowns, and busyness? Is there such a thing as responding and celebrating with an everyday faith?*

Vibrant faith, I assumed, was for people in ministry. You know, the *super*spiritual: those who have master of divinity degrees, or go to Israel in their spare time, or tell supermarket strangers about Jesus. Bless.their.hearts. I somehow couldn't erase the image of faith being like a childhood illusion of running through daisies, donned in an eyelet dress, chasing butterflies with God. I'm sorry, but I just can't pull off eyelet dresses these days. *Tell me, how does faith fit in with bills and cancer and feeling too much? How does God manifest through social media, the routine, and loneliness? For the kind of people like me, who have kids who whine, a marriage that demands work, and crazy passionate dreams? Is there space for that type of faith?*

Unsure, I did my best to pursue it.

I read the words and sang the songs. I smiled and served and poured myself into all things church and loving and others. And I was exhausted. Except I didn't know it.

I mistook intimacy with God as *my* responsibility. As though life was a party that I was in charge of planning. One where I had to do all the inviting, decorating, cooking, and making sure everything went flawlessly. If faith was an event, I'd set a lavish banquet table with my favorite china, flowering centerpieces, and tons of chairs. Oh.the.chairs. There were dozens, because this table was feeding the masses, friends. Frank Sinatra sang in the background, each course smelled like heaven, and the whole tablescape was Pinterest ideal. All was perfectly arranged until the unexpected came in various forms. Burnt food. A lull in the music. Empty chairs. This event I'd designed was not going as hoped, and I began doubting myself, God, and the serene story of what life as a Jesus follower should appear like.

I can't help but hope you understand. Is it safe to wonder if you relate to my disappointments and questions? I'm curious if you too, friend, have set expectations for life to go as a perfectly planned party. Do you envision the future with five-course meals, tons of guests, festive music, and fabulous champagne, and when no one shows up and the dinner gets cold and the evening doesn't go as anticipated, you start to wonder if this whole faith thing is a sham?

I'm here to tell you, it's not. How I wish I could plop you on my couch with an iced chai in one hand and a ginormous brownie in the other to look you in the eyes and whisper this: "You, my friend, you don't have to work so hard. You don't have to host the party and put out your best and cook for the masses. You don't have to strive to perform, because God is already in it. He is present right this very minute. He is using every aspect of the unplanned as an invitation for you to pause and enjoy Him first. Just you and your Father. He's offering space to meet. To get to know you. He wants to listen to your dreams and fears, to hold your hand and surprise you in out-of-the-box ways. He's inviting you to celebrate how *His* manifestations may look different from *your* expectations."

How will you choose to respond?

This is where choosing Real began for me. My dad's sudden passing became the catalyst to noticing how Jesus is more authentic than I had ever before experienced. As I stepped into the pain of loss, into foggy weeks of numbness and standing outside of my body, life shifted. They say suffering does that, and it's entirely true. *And* freeing. Alone with my thoughts, I recognized self-made habits I'd built around control.

Perhaps if I host more, work harder, or make this person feel special, I'll feel better. The only bummer was that I no longer *cared.* I was done fighting. I was over manufacturing a perfect faith. I was relinquishing my agenda.

As I hunched over with my legs folded on our weathered patio bench, for the first time, I *was.* I didn't *do.* I simply *existed.*

I'm done, God, I cried. *I'm tired. I have nothing to give anyone. Especially You.*

These feeble confessions changed my dependency on control. For the first time, I released all my people-pleaser, perfection-aspiring goals, the to-do lists, and faces I strived to make happy, and I got real down and dirty with my Lord. Getting real with Him saved my life. He drew me into safe corners I hadn't known were tangible. Into foreign spaces I'd ignored all my life. Suddenly I was keenly aware that every circumstance, person, and feeling is an invitation to see God's genuine heart in the middle of it.

Choosing Real is opting to see how present Jesus is in real-life circumstances. *Choosing Real* isn't about putting on one's big-girl panties. It's not about being strong, pep talking, or reciting the words "Let's do this." *Choosing Real* trusts God has a beautiful plan *in* the mess, *in* the scary, *in* the unknown, *in* the tears, and *in* not feeling enough.

When I ceased fighting and released myself to Him, when I curled up in the crook of His arm and said, *"Okay, Jesus, I've given faith everything I have and realize I've come to the end of me."* He gently nodded. *"I'll take it from here. I'll take you through pits and peaks and fears and fun, and transform it all to a calm, confident joy, as you come to understand that I.am.love."*

Now I respond to busy schedules, loss, transition, social media, the days I don't feel beautiful, and all the detours in between as an invitation. *Will I choose to see how God is real in them?* As I get comfortable relinquishing my control for His plan, will I intentionally celebrate His peace offerings, however they come?

Faith offerings shift my perspective from *me* to *He*. One after another they come:

An invitation to respond to life with an intentional yes
An invitation to rest in the midst of a frantic schedule
An invitation to hope in the midst of pain
An invitation to claim a Jesus identity during transition
An invitation to beauty and worth when I feel anything
    but beautiful and worthy
An invitation to community in the midst of loneliness
An invitation to find freedom in an online culture
An invitation to deeper relationships in the midst of
    tension
An invitation to choose gratitude
An invitation to sharpen my five fabulous senses
An invitation to embrace the ho-hum of the everyday
An invitation to serve beyond myself
An invitation to shine with God's unconditional love

Do you want more from life? Yes? Woot! This is where I channel my inner cheerleader and shout, *"You can know Him this intimately, too."* He doesn't want you to think of a relationship with Him as *that thing over there* saved for special occasions. No, He is inviting you—even as you read these words or think about what's for dinner or wonder when those shoes are going on sale or ache for your parent's cancer or fret over why that one relationship is so awkward—to experience genuine connection through all those details. *You* matter, and *how* you respond to what goes on in your day-to-day life matters. And celebrating your trust in God, regardless of how large or small your plans are, matters.

    Authentic, I'm learning, is a synonym for *Jesus.*

    Authentic faith is not one I scribble on my to-do list and check off at the end of the day. Nor fake with nice words or agree with obligatory *shoulds*. Authentic faith is freeing, skyscraper-jumping scary, and humbly dependent on the one who wrote the overarching story. It always has been and always will be about Jesus.

About His love.

Often I live for mountaintop experiences when, practically, He invites in the simplest of moments, transforming my mind to view schedules, work, and responsibilities as a way to dance in the storm. When I choose to find Him in family, in imperfection, in honest words, and within the walls of my home, I find my faith steadied toward a focused, into-the-heart offer.

As I get real with Jesus, He becomes real to me. The deeper I opt to offer my fears and thoughts, admit my silly dreams, and ask Him about His character, the more I discover His loving arms, His Spirit at the heart of real life. And so I press on and invite you to journey with me, as we look at how He is present in the oh-so-normal stuff. God longs for us to experience Him today. *Right now.* At work, in the grocery aisle, surrounded by people who require attention, or wherever life throws curveballs. When I'm tempted to plan my days to resemble an epic party, I'm choosing to grasp, laugh over, cling to, cry about, and celebrate just how real He truly is.

And from here, all of life is breathed and exhaled.

1
RSVP YES

An Invitation to Respond to Life with an Intentional Yes

We must cease striving and trust God to provide what He thinks is best and in whatever time He chooses to make it available. But this kind of trusting doesn't come naturally. It's a spiritual crisis of the will in which we must choose to exercise faith.
— Charles R. Swindoll

He held up four dimpled fingers, and two sapphire oceans stared up at me. "For my birthday I want chocolate chip cookies and a dance party." I laughed. Of course he does, this kid who can barely contain his passion for life and love for people. Of course he was planning ahead for his birthday, which happened to be six months from then.

My thoughts drifted to his first birthday celebration: *Ty & Tapas*. Both great-grandmas had called to clarify. "A topless party, Bekah? Really? What *is* this?" I explained about tapas—small plate, Spanish nibbles—and that in all honesty, it was a party for the adults, especially us parents, because, *Praise Jesus*, we survived his first year. "Please Grandma, come. And puhleeze, do wear a shirt."

I snapped to the present. "Cookies and a dance party sound perfect!"

Fall came, and Ty was in charge of the guest list and spouted off friends' names as fast as I could write them down.

At the bottom of the online invitation, four tiny letters sealed the deal: RSVP. Depending on whether people responded *yes* or *no* would affect the birthday celebration. For those who chose yes, cookies and sweet dance moves awaited—and the assurance their children would be sent home in a sugar coma. For the guests who couldn't attend, no problem— we'd understand. And for those who didn't respond to the invitation, it was just that.

It really couldn't get simpler than chocolate chip cookies and loud tunes and children dancing. Now, you must know, I'm impulsive and get overly excited about the smallest of events and may have gone a bit overboard on the baking. And because there is nothing, I repeat *nothing*, like a freshly baked chocolate chip cookie, let's not stop at a dozen. No, friend, let's make 150 homemade chocolate chip cookies—just in case the entire state of California responded positively to the birthday invite. As Tanner and Ty helped crack eggs, stir dry ingredients, and pour buckets of chocolate morsels into the mixer, my husband, Bryan, created an upbeat dance party mix, and we chatted about the upcoming birthday festivities. RSVPs came one after another: *Yes. Yes. Yes.*

Ty's birthday celebration was perfectly uncomplicated. Minimal setup. Unhindered time. Platters upon platters of homemade chocolate chip cookies. "Happy Birthday to You" voices in unison. Birthday boy basking. No-cares-in-the-world dancing. Loud music drawing in the neighbors.

Billy, from down the street, stopped by with his dog, watched on the outskirts, and left with a bag of cookies. From the driveway across, kids paused their game of basketball to bust a move and sample birthday treats. "Come on over," we invited neighbors. "Come dance and eat and celebrate." And some said yes while others stayed indoors. Long after guests left, our family sat on worn beach blankets and watched the sky entertain with her generous scoops of sherbet piled high in cloud bowls.

Have you ever noticed the opposing perspective between when you *host* and when you *attend* a party? When we RSVP *yes* to an invitation, we simply get to come and be. We don't have to buy the napkins, hang the banners, or nudge the final sheet of cookie dough balls into the oven, timing them perfectly for guests to savor warm treats. We simply come to enjoy. To relax and be included in the celebration. It requires little work on our part other than showing up and walking through the doors. The rest is soaking up laughter, savoring appetizers and fizzy drinks, shaking to catchy tunes, and breathing easy as kids run and squeal in utter joy. RSVPing *yes* means we experience an invitation to its fullest.

Growing up, I desperately wanted to say yes to the invitation of a dynamic relationship with Jesus. But I wondered how because no one ever explained to me that I didn't have to work so stinkin' hard at it. I concluded Christianity was nice people doing nice things for one another. I believed Jesus was who He said He was, but He always seemed a bit too perfect for me. I couldn't relate. I suppose deep in my gut I couldn't grasp that Jesus is actually personal and wanted to hang out with my feelings, my insecurities, and *me*. In high school I went on every church mission trip and volunteered for leadership roles in school and ministry, but my faith was performance based. I didn't understand I had a choice in allowing Jesus to take the lead. Because, *heaven forbid*, what if He didn't? How could I follow a Jesus I didn't have a real relationship with other than what I did *for* Him?

Until my early thirties, I lived out my faith the same way I lived out my natural calling—as the host, the inviter. Mostly because that's my sweet spot. I adore opening our cottage doors and welcoming friends with the clink of a glass and music dancing from the kitchen. Hosting families and encouraging them to feel cozy within our safe walls awakens me to my creative self. But I had a misguided belief that *physically* inviting people into my heart and home transferred into *spiritually* inviting. Thus the lie rooted: I was responsible to do the inviting with God. This unrealistic faith perspective was a heavy weight, one that put me in the center, doing all of the work.

Perhaps if I entertained Jesus enough, caught His attention, proved *why* He should attend my so-called party called *Bekah's life*, He would come. Hopefully with dessert. So I invited Him, but only to the major events. *God, will You join me on this mission trip? Can I get Your opinion on what college to attend? What are Your thoughts about my future spouse? Career? Where should we live?* On and off, I used Him like a seasonal accessory.

Jesus the hat.

Jesus the cute scarf.

Jesus the sassy neon belt.

Mostly, I asked Him to meet me in the important parts of life because I didn't know how to be real about mundane, unexciting details. Like *How do I navigate friendships in college? Where are You when it comes to my shifting identity?* It barely crossed my mind that He would want to listen to my heartache or family tension or marital spats. And because I didn't know how to invite Him into the oh-so-normal parts of my life, doubt took hold. Deep, dark doubt. If I wasn't aware of how to be personal with Him, there was no way I could conceive that He wanted to know me, all of me, every nook and cranny. Sure, I knew Christianity claimed that Jesus wanted an intimate relationship with me, but practically grasping it was another story.

I heard little discussion of life not going as planned from the older generation, from people at church, from the pulpit. *Will someone explain how real life collides with faith? How do I respond with my temporal circumstances and let God use them for His eternal plan? And how does this whole faith thing work in the everyday?*

Unsure, I decided, *I'll keep on keeping on. I'll connect with Jesus when I read my Bible. I'll carve out space when I'm not working or chasing my little monkeys around or trying to make sense of life. I'll do it all even if I'm worn out. And I'll do it with a smile, because that's what faith looks like.* Adamant foot stomp.

Come. The more the merrier. I invited and planned and hosted. At the core, I recognized a frantic inner fan. *Whir, whir, whir.* The unceasing white noise begged me to pause. Little did I know it was God's Spirit, beckoning me to follow, to stop whirring about, and give Him space and time to initiate a relationship with me. If I'm honest, at the center was fear. Fear that if I stopped reaching out and organizing, I wouldn't be accepted, thought of, or invited. So I took control and used my natural gift for connection but suffocated it beneath panic and charged ahead.

Yes, I choose You, God. But I mapped out life on my own. He would place dreams in my heart and mind, but I'd stress about what would happen if I went for them and failed. I had friends but was afraid I wasn't enough for them. I was real with others about hard times, but did I really believe God wanted to endure my brain chatter?

What does it look like to respond to Jesus' invitation for a genuine relationship with Him?

First, I have to believe He *wants* to invite me—all of me. If I can't wholeheartedly embrace how He sees me, knows all my crazy thoughts, and right this moment is planning the menu and pouring glasses, then I can't take the next step. Only when my head connects to my heart and I know with every fiber in me that He is already here and chooses me, then, and only then, can I move forward.

With trust established, I now have a basic choice—do I respond *yes* or *no*? Do I trust my unknown to God more than I trust my sense of control? More than my outcome and plan? Do I choose to enter into an expectant posture, or do I choose a five-step, fill-in-the-blank, paint-by-number life? Saying *yes* views every feeling, experience, relationship, and bump in the road as an opportunity to see from His vantage point. *Yes* holds plans open, turns palms up, and acknowledges that God knows what He's doing. Responding with a nod means, *Lord, how can I get closer to Your heart through this?* The reality is that when I constantly did the initiating with others (and sometimes even with God), doing so became tiring. Exhausting. I secretly wanted to fling my arms out wide, tilt my head back, and give up. I wanted to stop trying to make sense of details and allow God to take over.

But wait. What if *I* can let God do the inviting? What if *you* can let Him? Let Him send the invitations, plan the event, choose the colors and theme and guest list as He comes to celebrate us? What if we let Him lay out the dreams He has placed within us since before time in the order He knows best? What if we choose to know He is weaving passion and pain and grace so personally together that it *has* to be journeyed with Him to appreciate His peace all the more? What if it starts with one lip-quivering *yes*?

Bob Goff, a life-embracing communicator and world changer, in his guttural laugh type of way, said, "Every day God invites us on the same kind of adventure. It's not a trip where He sends us a rigid itinerary; He simply invites us. God asks what it is He's made us to love, what it is that captures our attention, what feeds that deep indescribable need of our souls to experience the richness of the world He made. And then, leaning over us, He whispers, 'Let's go do that together.'"[1] This invitation visual makes my heart happy.

Slowly, my perspective shifts. Before I assumed the role of inviter, but now I receive hundreds, thousands of daily invitations to follow and join Him. The invitations can come like they did when I was a child in the traditional sense of His black-and-white words found in scripture. They come through prayer and people. But they also surprise deeply as God's Spirit sprinkles out-of-the-box invitations through dreams, my children, nature, and music. I notice His offer as I'm baking, designing, playing with our sons, as the sun sinks into the silver ocean. Wise souls tell us, and they are correct, that the harder the circumstance, the clearer He becomes.

His invitations arrive.

A crisp white envelope with black bold script. *"Will you choose to trust Me with this job interview?"*

A crumpled, tearstained envelope with smeared pen. *"Will you choose to follow Me into the unknown of this move away from family?"*

A small, dark envelope with faint type. *"Will you choose to follow Me when you feel alone?"*

A dazzling gold envelope on the screen. *"Will you choose to follow Me when marriage is hard work and everyone else on Instagram looks like they have it together?"*

A formal envelope with numbers signifying a patient's name. *"Will you choose to follow Me when your dad has cancer?"*

The choices come, one after another, carrying extreme feelings and real-life circumstances, and I get to rip open the pretty, ugly, and scary packaging to peer inside. Only I can respond to each and every invitation. Will I RSVP *yes* or *no*?

God's Spirit beckons, presenting a choice to create my own path, even under the mask of faith—or to recognize Him as the Inviter, the One Who Has Already Shown Up. As Ulrich Henn, a German sculptor, so beautifully said, "All men, believing in God or not, are invited to enter. I wish to make them curious to see what God has to offer them within the cathedral."[2] Here lies my choice: *Will I enter into where God is inviting?*

Oh friend, how backward my perspective used to be. This trust journey *is* an invitation, one that begins with God first inviting me. Inviting me to come with my fears and questions and stories of transition and pain. Inviting me to carry broken dreams, an imperfect family, and fragile expectations. Inviting me to bring my bags packed with life's experiences, which He so willingly offers to carry. He invites me to RSVP to this faith journey. To let Him surprise me in the order, the people, and the gifts wrapped in pain. He is a giver of good gifts, but I have to trust He knows *when* and *how* and *why* to give them. And believe He remains constantly Real even when gifts are taken away.

Too often I still try to host. To take control and design the menu, coordinate the napkins to fit with the theme, and *Hmmm, what games should we play? Favors or no favors?* No wonder I wore myself thin. I perceived faith much in the same way as a party I planned. Every new sunrise offers opportunities to respond *yes*. Will I see how God is Real in *this* circumstance, *this* emotion, and *this* relationship? Will I choose to engage, despite how painful or lonely or awkward doing so may be? Or will I try to host?

Bryan and I love inviting, but how great is our joy when we are invited. Thought of by people who want to know us more. Esteemed enough to be welcomed into their homes. Being invited is one of the most humbling gifts to receive because it has nothing to do with us making the event happen and everything to do with showing up and choosing to be seen.

In his book *Yes or No: How Your Everyday Decisions Will Forever Shape Your Life*, Jeff Shinabarger talks about community and noticing people enough to invite them, especially when they are withdrawing. He wrote, "If you see people you care about retreating, engage them. They need you. They need your care, your listening ear, and your perspective to help them through whatever has them stuck. We were made for each other."[3] How true this is for community but even more so for how Jesus longs to invite us into community with Him.

What does it look like to say yes to God? To greet Him as the Welcomer? To let Him intentionally place people to intersect your journey while they travel their specific paths?
"Come enjoy and taste and see and experience," God says.

When I attend God's party with my fears about being too emotional and my ginormous, passionate dreams, He asks me to bring them all—the whole shebang. He welcomes my heart for others, my honest frustrations about busy schedules, and my hope to be intentional in my parenting of our curious boys. When I RSVP *yes*, I'm saying yep to every last drop, His realness in each and every situation. RSVPing *yes* is a good starting point.

When Jesus invites, when He shows up and knocks gently, when He whispers through classmates and coworkers, co-op moms and crazy calendars, we have the choice to accept and walk through the door with Him or to continue putting on the "inviter hat." We know how it feels to be invited in, so why do we so often refuse these invitations and go about our way, hoping He'll ask later when we're less busy?

It took my son's birthday party to surface deep faith questions. *Will I RSVP to Jesus' invitation to follow Him, even when I'm not sure what that even means? Will I choose to grab hold of His hand while my other arm carries bags of real-life questions? Will I recognize that in the moments when I question, "Is there more? Is this it?" followed by my most honest confession, "I hope there's more," that God* is *here? That He is meeting, waiting, and patiently holding out His hand?*

Of course, God starts with an invitation, an offering of Himself. On the cross Jesus invited me to follow. And since then His invitations haven't ceased. No wonder He starts by meeting me where I am in my current season. An invitation is by far the most beautiful expression of love and grace. It requires no work on my part other than acceptance. His invitation includes all of life, every dark corner and every vibrant, celebratory space.

As I respond with the nodding of my head and grasping of Jesus' hand, I notice the change. No longer do I have to host, plan, and invite my faith into existence. No longer do I have to view this temporary life, this one shot at enjoying Jesus and others on earth, as though it's on my shoulders. No, real life is a journey of following Him who knows the plan, by seeing every life aspect through His eternal lens. Now I am free to put aside my tendency to work toward faith and instead choose to walk through the first circumstance of His offer by simply saying *yes*.

Yes, Jesus, I choose You. I choose to say yes to Your invitation into this oh-so-real journey. I choose to see You in frantic schedules and a perfection-projecting online culture. I choose to follow You into transition and pain and expectations. When I feel loneliness, tension, the unexpected, and numbing grief, may I see how You transform every situation so that it has an eternal focus. When I say yes, Jesus, I want to be real with You in my parenting, my anxiety, and my insecurity. I want to see life differently. No longer do I want to view my hours through a foggy perspective but through Your lens. Jesus, You invite me onto a personal faith path. Along the way I will face uncomfortable situations, mundane routines, self-doubts, and challenging conversations, but as You ask me to come, to sit on Your couch and be real with You first, You transform my temporal view into an eternal perspective. You invite me to celebrate life the way You intended.

Real life begs the invitation to follow Jesus. In each season of faith, I have a choice to agree that He knows best and trust His perspective or to do things on my own. I've done things on my own—even if it appeared as though I was trusting Him. By following Him into the real stuff, the true grit, He transforms the tiniest of details and the darkest of valleys, drawing me closer to His heart.

And He holds out His hand and invites us to follow. Dance parties included.

Will you RSVP with an intentional yes?

Ty's Fourth Birthday "Dance Party" Playlist

Disclaimer: This ain't your "Jesus Loves Me" playlist. Some songs may have sassy words or lyrics. Ain't no perfection here. Dance on.

"Life Is a Highway," Rascal Flatts
"I Gotta Feeling," Black Eyed Peas
"Party Rock Anthem," LMFAO
"Kung Fu Fighting," CeeLo Green
"Everything Is Awesome," Tegan and Sara
"Shake It Off," Taylor Swift
"I Can't Help Myself," Four Tops
"Hey Ya!" OutKast
"Love You Like a Love Song," Selena Gomez & the Scene
"What Does the Fox Say?" Ylvis
"Feel This Moment," Pitbull
"Roar," Katy Perry
"When Can I See You Again?" Owl City
"Teenage Mutant Ninja Turtles Theme Song," Teenage Mutant Ninja Turtles

---

2
ENJOY THE JOURNEY

An Invitation to Rest in the Midst of a Frantic Schedule

Rest is not idleness, and to lie sometimes on the grass under trees on a summer's day, listening to the murmur of the water, or watching the clouds float across the sky, is by no means a waste of time.
—John Lubbock, *The Use of Life*

*R*ed leaves waft like mini stop signs, arranging themselves at my feet, on the sidewalk, blinking a path to the car as the boys and I jump inside and pull buckles across chests and laps. As summer shifts to fall, autumn's attire whispers of God's hint to slow down. Fiery persimmon hues and burnt-yellow shades beckon notice as brave Miss Liquidambar Tree cautions, *Stop. Look around. It's that time of year when you begin to push yourself ragged. Here's a warning: fall needn't equal hectic frenzy; it hints of rest and self-care.*

It's taken me years to listen to wise Miss Ambar.

Ironically, faith lessons are built through the very circumstances I'm madly trying to control. Frequently fall signals busyness, crammed schedules, and *more, more, more.* Yet I push familiar undertones of craving *stillness* aside.

As if the first ER visit wasn't enough to freak any parent out. No stranger to croup episodes, Ty's usually come on in .2 seconds, and when, from down the hall, we heard him barking, we kicked into amateur crazy-parents-save-son mode. Into the bathroom. Shower on full heat. "Breathe in, buddy," we urged. Ty's quick gasps came, and Bryan and I found ourselves holding our breath until he took his next. "He's turning blue," I whispered. Since he wasn't auditioning for the part of Willy Wonka's Violet in his transitional kindergarten class, that alone urged us to call the fire department, who dispatched paramedics. This is where I pause to tell you that in those few minutes between the call and his blue, gasping for air episode, Ty had a miraculous healing. When five firefighters appeared at our doorstep ready to save a child, Ty answered the door to welcome new friends inside for a midnight playdate.

I could have croaked.

Ty, you're supposed to be dying, I thought nervously. Yellow-uniformed men smiled, checked him out, gifted him a stuffed animal, and offered us the choice of them taking him to the hospital or driving him ourselves. Since "we'd rather be safe than sorry," Bryan took him to the ER while I stayed home with Tanner, who miraculously slept through the entire ordeal (I confess sleep envy focused at our older son).

This, my friend, is how our fall began, a flurry of new beginnings, of *firsts.*

First days of school for the boys. *First* soccer practices, which Bryan—bless his heart—volunteered to *first-time* coach in addition to full-time pastoring. I was speaking, writing for our church's storytelling department, and attempting to master, *What exactly does a soccer mom do these days?* There were midweek practices, Saturday games, and uniform washing. And apparently orange slices and Gatorade snacks are so twenty years ago. These days creative parents emerge with brightly colored monogrammed satchels overflowing with crackers, Evian water, and enough food to ensure my son won't want to eat dinner until 10:00 p.m. Mouth-open amazed, I seriously applaud the folks who excel at soccer snacks but must warn you: if your child is on our son's team, our family *will* gift him orange slices and a Gatorade. In a crumpled brown bag. *Cue cheesy smile.*

So, yes. We were ~~adjusting~~ surviving to a fresh fall, declaring on repeat, "This is a *first* for us."

The ER visit being our first.

Until the following weekend, when a second ER snafu manifested. This time it was my mom who called, as she'd graciously offered to watch our boys so Bryan and I could attend a friend's birthday where tacos and a margarita bar fed dozens. I do believe there was a game of Bunco that I got in trouble for socializing at instead of following the rules. Li'l Mom's call interrupted to break the bad news. "Umm, Ty has these weird, oozy sores on his face and back, and he's complaining they hurt."

Turns out my sweet husband—I do adore him so—befriended a homeless man when he and Ty were in the ER waiting room the week before. "Yeah, he had some sores on him, but he was sitting next to us, so I shook his hand," Bry said with a shrug.

"What? Stop trying to love on everyone," I scolded. "I mean seriously, it's like you're a pastor at heart." Oh wait.

"Ty, welcome to the ER Take 2. You have impetigo. Yes, it sounds like a native disease, but it's really a fancy way of saying you have oozy sores on your face. Please don't touch them. They are contagious and spread when you even think about another human." *Gag.*

It was during these fabulous *firsts* that I sensed God

inviting me to rest. *"Bekah, just be. Take time for your soul. Rest. Rest. Rest."*

I wanted to throw a pillow at the Lord, I was so dang frustrated with His request. Yet I knew, in quiet pockets where my soul craved recharge and peace, that rest was exactly what I needed.

But how? How does one truly rest in the midst of life all around? With school drop-off, homework, relationships, and work? When bills and deadlines require attention and time? Sure, I can plan my part; I can cut oranges for soccer games and gas the car and open my heart to a million questions our boys bring in from the day. But my life never goes as anticipated.

This life I'm attempting to control, this party I'm desperately hoping to create, is not getting the memo. Where I envision a perfectly orchestrated event, a five-course menu, a chef cooking foodie magic, his team reading his moves so that every course is plated in a timely fashion, it's overrun by rush, throwing everything out of whack. This gourmet meal ends up scrambled. The main course is scorched, appetizers linger behind the salad, and dessert shows up at the table first. *And is something burning?* Busyness begets charred plans. Singed hopes. Smoky visions. Ideals are peppered with ruined menu items. *Why isn't anything going as expected?*

Never mind that our family is on a first-name basis with the local ER staff.

I find myself unaware of a need until I take a quiet moment to listen. To *Him*. When distractions are at a pause—whether at home on the couch after a long day of work, or when the kids are settled into bed, or when my mind actually has a minute to shake hands with itself—I notice that quiet stirring. But then the pull to slow down is interrupted by my need to keep going, keep cleaning, keep doing.

The Sunday after our second ER visit, I jumped from bed, thrilled we'd escaped an ER visit before the stroke of midnight the eve before, only to land on puke from our beloved shih tzu while simultaneously hearing Tanner's shrill voice vibrating from his room.

"*Moooom*, you better come here." I walked into an ideal setting, where brothers sat side by side on their rug building with Legos.

"C'mon guys, let's get dressed. We actually get to go to church this morning, and we're getting *doughnuts*." I'm singing at this point, unsure of who is more excited about the doughnut idea.

Ty looked up and, with the sweetest angel voice, proudly stated, "Mom, I put a Lego up my nose."

You guys. I went into denial.

"No you didn't, silly. You're fine. I'm sure it's a small Lego. It'll wiggle its way out. Ya know, build character in those nose muscles of yours." Somehow this was all making sense in my mind. *I'll just pull it out, and we'll be on our way.*

Channeling my inner MacGyver, I looked to Tanner as my sidekick.

I laid Ty on his bottom bunk and offered an open palm to our oldest. "Flashlight," I ordered. Tanner placed a small light in my hand.

Shining it up my youngest's schnoz, I saw it. *Barely.* A tiny, almost translucent, round Lego. If tweezers chased after it, his brains would surely spill out.

So I did what a mom at the end of her wits does. I yelled and screamed and had a tiny tantrum.

Is it too much to ask for one normal weekend? One Sunday

we can actually go to church 'cuz we weren't at the ER the entire night before? Doughnuts, people. We had plans to eat doughnuts this morning.

I called my hubby at church, snorting into the receiver, and informed him, "I will be delivering our oldest child to you, and will you please find me another ER that is outside of the greater Orange County area?"

Wasn't this the season to conquer rest? *Bahaha. 'Rest,' you mocking four-letter word.*

But here's the thing. What do you think of when I ask you about rest? About soul care?

If you're like me, you immediately think of sleep. Maybe hibernation. I love asking this question to women, because ninety-nine percent of the time, sleep is the first answer they give, with the exception of one woman triumphantly shouting, "Retirement!"

Oh gosh. I don't want to wait until I retire to get some much-needed peace. And that is why, as I entered into this quest for self-care and rest, I was struck by how I was focusing on the wrong definition.

There are several definitions of rest but only one with which I most connect. Rest can be "freedom from activity or labor," which is impossible if one is breathing. It is also defined as "a state of motionlessness or inactivity," which translates to death. There's rest, as in "a place for lodging" like the Four Seasons or a fancy shmancy hotel that most of us escape to on an anniversary or rare getaway. And then my eyes land on the last definition of rest: "peace of mind or spirit."

Did your shoulders immediately relax?

No wonder I used to scoff at the idea of rest. I was choosing to focus primarily on the physical meaning of rest, a meaning that isn't practical in the day-to-day. If rest is God's idea, surely He wouldn't tease us with the notion of it. His heart is never to shame but to offer peace in a life tempted to run frantically. To rest means to be filled up by the One who enjoys us right in the middle of the rush. Authentic rest emulates our Father; it's turning my mind and heart to settle into a cozy rhythm that models Him, even if a million dishes are flying about the kitchen.

As Ty and I sat in the waiting room, I texted Bryan, admitting silent curse words toward our youngest son, and truth came from my husband's reply, I'M PRAYING GOD WILL USE THIS EXPERIENCE TO SEE HIM IN IT.

Whatever.

Not one moment later did a family stumble through the sliding doors, a pajama-clad wife bent over, as her husband aided her steps and with his free hand held their toddler son. The woman had a blanket wrapped around and under her. Clearly she was miscarrying, and her eyes had that far-off look, one I've come to understand. One of throbbing, numbing pain.

They sat in the open seats next to us. Quiet. She fought back tears, and her husband attempted to distract the child while he rubbed his wife's knee. And here I was annoyed about a lame Lego.

Approaching us, their young son was curious about Ty's coloring book and crayons. "Do you want to share with him?" I whispered in Ty's ear. There are moments when God breaks through, holy and near, so personal I can hear His breath and sense His presence. In the middle of a crowded waiting room, He focused my rushed mind, stilling my thoughts and making me aware of His Real Self.

Ty drew close to the boy, offering his Ninja coloring book and a handful of crayons, and my eyes met the mom. We exchanged priceless silent words. "Thank you," she mouthed. "Thank you."

For a moment, I prayed that little boy wouldn't remember being afraid of waiting in the ER lobby while his mom clutched a blanket and his parents cried. I prayed he'd look back and remember coloring green Ninja Turtles with a new friend.

Rest. It comes through experiencing God's Spirit of peace when disruptions and ER visits and miscarriages distract my view and tempt me to focus on the chaos instead of His calm.

When circumstances are fun, viewed through skippy moments and rosy champagne flutes, I don't need peace. No, it's often in pain and waiting room unknowns; it's in suffering and darkness where God declares Himself and brings peace to our minds and spirits, because that's when we desperately need Him. No amount of fast-forwarding or busyness can create enough friction to launch us past needing peace. As long as there are waiting room seasons, we can either respond by wading through the mess or walking around it. Embracing or escaping.

Turns out Ty's Lego popped out easily *in addition to a BB he'd shoved up his other nostril.* (I know.) Pleased with his newfound attention, Ty held a pair of tiny spheres, smaller than peas, in cupped hands, while the doctor stood in front of me, her finger gently pointed in earnest.

"Ty," she cooed, "we do not put Legos or BBs or anything else up our nose. Okay?"

Without missing a beat, that stinker looked at her then

at me. Then he leaned forward, showing microscopic gifts in open palms, and said, "Next time, I'm going to shove the *house* up there."

And that, my friends, is why I need peace.

And prayer.

And rest.

It's no wonder God talks so much about rest in the Bible. In the Old Testament, rest was focused on the Sabbath, a day set aside when work was avoided and people were encouraged to worship and simply be. I love the concept but have trouble setting aside a whole day when no baking or work or dance parties occur. Thank the Lord for the New Testament. When His Son came, along with His Spirit, grace swept a refreshing second color across the canvas, magnifying rest where, before, legalism marked.

When I read Matthew 11:28–30 (NKJV), something deep within awakens. "Come to Me, all you who labor and are heavy laden, and I will give you rest. Take My yoke upon you and learn from Me, for I am gentle and lowly in heart, and you will find rest for your souls. For My yoke is easy and My burden is light."

Yes, please. "Easy" and "light" and "rest for your souls." I'll take a large helping of that, thank You, kind Sir.

Experiencing the type of peace that comes only from resting in Him is where I long to find myself—smack in the middle of nostril surprises and unplanned events. As I taste the value of rest, I don't want to go back to the urgency I led from before. I spent too many early married/young mommy years living in the ideal of the future or analyzing the past, neglecting to enjoy today—to be present to the tiny moments and memories making up the *who* and *what* texture of *now*.

In her faith memoir, *Leaving Church*, Barbara Brown Taylor confesses her addiction to busyness and how rest has forever transformed her. "Like many ambitious people, I had developed a dependence for adrenaline. I could get so much done when my anxiety was in the red zone that I learned to live right on the edge of panic, in that optimum zone between alarm and collapse. It was my version of running hurdles and I was good at it."[4] Ultimately her exhaustion propelled her to step away from her priesthood at an Episcopalian parish. She learned how to sit for more than twenty minutes "without fearing my head would explode." She learned how to breathe deeply, as a woman rested, not rushed, and "when the air came back out of me again, it did not emerge like air escaping through the pinched neck of a rubber balloon. It emerged as the sigh of a rested person, which I had not been for quite some time."[5]

How do you know if you're a rested person? Perhaps the best barometer is a mirror to reflect where rest is absent. Are you tired? Anxious? Stressed? Do you have headaches? When I'm not rested, I bite at my family and have no patience to draw from. What I pull up are frantic attempts to control all situations. Peace can't be found apart from God's Spirit.

The Holy Spirit's invitation comes, even in a children's classic. Tanner and I finished reading *Charlotte's Web*, a nightly tradition where he snuggled close under a blanket and watched my finger follow sentences. From time to time he looked up with a question or giggle. We came to the part where Charlotte told Wilbur, "Never hurry and never worry."

"Stop, Mom." Tanner sat up. "Read that again."

"Never hurry and never worry." Children's books are abundant with truth, and this one hit me at the core.

If worry is a symptom, hurried life's root is control. Somewhere along the journey of growing up, we went from being cared for to taking care of others. We neglected the middle part, where we opt to be cared for by the Soul Nourisher in order to care for others. When I live being filled *first*, caretaking is life giving, not exhausting.

When I was a young girl, my father's famous phrase practically smiled as it exited his lips. "Enjoy the journey," he beamed. Born in a hurry, I rolled my eyes, probably on my way out the door. *Ya, ya, Dad. Whatever.*

Decades later, age and maturity are teaching me how valuable those three words are. My soul longs for that very understanding—to enjoy the journey. But how? What does that look like in the rush? In the busy? In the responsibilities and demands of life and little ones?

Philippians 4:6–7 says, "Do not be anxious about anything, but in everything by prayer and supplication with thanksgiving let your requests be made known to God. And the *peace* of God, which surpasses all understanding, will guard your hearts and your minds in Christ Jesus" (esv, emphasis added). *A* to the *men*.

Friends, hear this: Rest is not selfish; it is essential. It is biblical. When fall greets, red leaves blink warnings—not to *physically* stop but to focus *mind* and *heart* toward Jesus-offering peace. The suggestion is perspective awareness. An offer to peer through circumstances even when they fly at warp speed. To embrace rest and inner peace. Serenity *among* the crazy. Isn't that what we desire? Not to cancel life, move to a mountain, and claim stillness, but to really know Jesus' genuine heart, where calm is obtainable in the hustle-bustle of humanity.

I know a woman, Tiffany, who I bumped into more than

a decade after attending the same college together. And boy, is she a fan of self-care. With four kids, a husband who works for his father's business, living in the country, she proudly shares, "I need 'me time' every morning." And then she lives it out. She gets up early and goes to the gym, comes home, gets her kids breakfast, and unashamedly lets them watch a show or movie while she reads, journals, prays, *whatever* it is that fills her up, knowing she will empty the remainder of her day. She feels off when she misses her consistent rest rhythm. Do you know what's inspiring about her story? She claims her worth in needing rest, because she believes she is worthy of finding peace to start her day. She fights for it and knows that without space carved out each morning, she, her marriage, and her kids *will* suffer.

In response to valuing rest, these are the questions I'm asking and five practices I'm embracing to seek calm in the midst of a *go, go, go* schedule. If it's peace you crave, I invite you on a rest journey alongside.

1. ***Believe your value comes in who you are, not what you do.***
When my identity is secured in a God of grace and love, everything overflows from an inner worth, not an outer work. Where do you go for value? Do you spend it first with Jesus or offer Him the leftovers? I admit, I used to give Him the extra minutes (*ba-ha*—when are there *ever* extra minutes?). Ironically, the extra minutes are never enough to recoup after a harried day. No, it has to come before my feet hit the carpet. It starts with, *God, help me not miss You today.*

At our core is the need to be loved. To be enjoyed by God first. When the kids are asleep or you find yourself day-dreaming on the job, does the question *Who am I?* simmer?

I know it sounds obvious, but when I lose myself to God's Spirit, I find my truest self. In Exodus 33:14, the Lord said to Moses, "My Presence will go with you, and I will give you rest" (ESV). If it's peace I desire, I have to spend time in His presence. Simple truth. Challenging application.

When I think about my favorite people, the ones I can't wait to make breakfast plans with or get a babysitter for the kids so we can connect over happy hour, it's because I love spending time with them. Afterward we walk away feeling refreshed, seen, known. So it is with time with God. Maybe it's not on a mountain but in a laundry pile. What would it look like to rid yourself of the box you believe God has to meet you in, and instead choose to let Him enjoy you for who you are?

2. ***Do something every day that makes each of your five senses come alive in ways that encourage you to find peace in your created self.***

I'm a firm believer that God is fun, and it's my controlling perspective that imagines Him as a stern grandpa with a long beard. What if rest can be fun, too?

Each day, I make it a goal to sway to music while packing lunches or doing errands. Some days it's Adele; other days it's worship or Coldplay. He's in it. All.

A friend of mine is in the toddler trenches, and she called, stressed. "Throw those babes in the car and drive through Starbucks and treat yourself to your favorite drink," I encouraged her. "Who says peace can't be obtained from a dirty chai, extra espresso, please?"

To tap into the visual senses, I leave scripture reminders in sight, read inspiring books and blogs, and frame faith-filled quotes. Okay, I get a bit out of control and Post-it my office and lipstick the bathroom mirrors, but what I read is what I believe, so why not wallpaper my kitchen with peace-aspiring reminders? (I'm imagining a season of *Hoarders* at this point.)

Wear something that makes you feel beautiful. Lip gloss and a chunky necklace do wonders for the soul.

Express yourself creatively. Over the summer, our family built a back patio swing. Swinging provides remarkable therapy for kids with ADHD and people with anxiety. Our family? We just plain love to swing. On summer nights, Bryan and I sit out there, wine in hand, a safe, cozy seat to rest.

When I threw out the question "How do you embrace self-care?" to my readers, their responses echoed life-giving ways to experience peace: yoga at night, reading, leaving their computers at work, carving out a soul care day, running (you will never hear me say that, but I have the utmost respect for all my running peeps). When we choose to invest in life-giving sensory activities, God invites us to understand His peace in a more textured and broader scope.

3. ***When you feel overwhelmed, ask yourself,* Am I sacrificing my sanity or family to make this happen?**

Join me as we stand back and pray about how God wants us to spend our time. I can't do it all. What is His best for me? For my marriage? For my family? For you and yours? Creating healthy boundaries removes my control talons and anchors them with freeing permission. Along with God's prompting, only I am in charge of my calendar. Yet when those evites and school invitations and Bible study sign-ups and fabulous opportunities present themselves like an all-you-can-eat buffet, my inner idealist shouts, *Yes! I'll do it all.* (Been there?) Then one by one, everyone suffers.

In her rockstar book *For the Love*, Jen Hatmaker lays out the basic idea that if life were a pie, us gals believe we need to excel in every.single.slice. In the past, ladies didn't run frantic trying to outdo themselves in every facet of human possibility. Somewhere along the journey, though, we've come to believe that we must provide Disneyland-ish experiences for our children; invest in our personal giftings; have a world-impacting calling; maintain Pinterest abodes and *Better Homes & Gardens* yards; cook organic gourmet meals; make sure all relationships are poured into; keep our marriage red.hot.passionate; embrace self-care; minister to church, neighbors, universe; and actively deepen our faith through Bible studies *and* hosting small groups in spotless, chaos-free homes.

We simply can't do it all, and I am so thankful He doesn't expect us to.

It was after the third ER visit that I knew I had to protect a day in my week to refill, to be poured *into* so I can pour *out*. When I began this rhythm, I became aware of how many years I neglected to honor soul care as a necessary part of my schedule. When had I become so focused on ignorantly sacrificing myself? Mondays, the first course, now mark the week's rhythm, starting with fill, pour, work, play. Park walks fill. Writing fills. Blasting worship music and listening to my Creator's voice while I bake brownies fills. Designing our home and holding babies fills. I have to first fill before I have any energy to work.

Maya Angelou shared her heart's need to get away to fill.

Every person needs to take one day away. A day in which one consciously separates the past from the future. Jobs, family, employers, and friends can exist one day without any one of us, and if our egos permit us to confess, they could exist eternally in our absence. Each person deserves a day away in which no problems are confronted, no solutions searched for. Each of us needs to withdraw from the cares which will not withdraw from us.[6]

So I gobble up rest windows when they open—often in the shower. I know friends who put down their phones when they nurse and listen to the stillness of a babe. Others drive to the grocery store, windows down, listening to the wind's whispers. If it's rest we need to live fully, it's the minutes we must enjoy, for those are when God shows up.

4. *Listen to your body.*

Do you find that your mind never stops? Do you wake with your heart jackhammering in your chest? Is your skin breaking out? Stress plays a pivotal role in pointing toward the value of rest. We each have twenty-four hours in a day. How will you choose to invest in yours?

I had the honor of returning to my alma mater, Azusa Pacific University, to share with the freshman class about transitions. Afterward, a transfer student, about twenty years old, approached and shared her story. As a young woman, she had endured not one but *two* types of cancer. Always the strong one, she confessed she held her family and friends together. "I've never even cried since I was diagnosed." Tight lips hinted at sheer fatigue, and I wrapped my arm around hers.

"Are you exhausted?" I whispered. From her left eye, the

first tear fell, then from her right eye, another, until she was staring back, her lips shaking. "I've done such a good job building walls around myself. Trying to be strong for everyone else."

I related to her story, noting my control-prone temperament wrapped in "helpfulness" for others. In that moment, I knew the greatest words I could share were of my own heartbeat. "What would it look like," I asked as I hugged her, "to let God hold you for a while?" She e-mailed me later to tell me she'd made a counseling appointment and had a good cry. She is on her way to experiencing rest that comes only from the Father. She is embarking on the truth journey in 2 Corinthians 12:9–10: when we are weak, God is strong.

5. *Allow yourself to be enjoyed*.

It was at the Serra Retreat Center in Malibu that I experienced the gift of being enjoyed. Looking out over the mossy valley, I made myself comfortable on a Spanish tile bench with apple slices and a writing pad and asked God a simple yet bold question. If I hadn't had paper and pen handy, to this day, I wouldn't recall words that spoke enjoyment arrows to my tired soul.

What I "Heard" on a Silent Retreat

Hey, God, would you mind sharing something, Ya know, from a heavenly Father to a daughter?

I enjoy YOU.

Huh? Really? 'Cuz I'm kinda cranky today
and I don't forgive enough.
I'm better at apologizing to my kids than I
am to my spouse,
and I feel unmotivated many days.

I enjoy YOU.

That's nice, but I'm not good at making meals
when people have babies.
I don't currently serve at church.
I should call and check on friends more
and tidy less and jump on the trampoline
with the boys when they ask.

I enjoy YOU.

You sure? Because there are so many people
more talented,
more visible, more creative,
who have greater gifts and are smarter than I.

I enjoy YOU.

But I'm impulsive and passionate
and quick to start and slow to finish.
I want to appear more polished than the
tangled knots I feel inside.
I wish I wasn't as sensitive or analytical.

I enjoy YOU.

Me? Just as I am? In process? Super messy?
Learning how to forgive and love unconditionally?
Wrestling to know Your heart in a
multimessage-shouting world?
You enjoy me just like this?

Yes. I enjoy YOU.

I learned a pivotal lesson that day on the cliffs of Malibu: I am enjoyed by the Creator of the universe.

You are enjoyed by the Creator. Just.as.you.are.

And His peace doesn't come when we cancel our calendars and sit alone on a mountain. If it did, I wouldn't be interested in that kind of faith. What I crave is understanding a Creator who crashes into real life in real time through everyday offerings. *Do you sense Him drawing you to rest in His presence even now?*

May we rest in that truth.
Find peace in His words.
Crave time in His presence.

Even as we sit on blankets and cheer kids at soccer, write business plans, and steam veggies, He's here. When goose bumps hint at crisp nights approaching, when fall waves her branches in red splendor, I pause. I stop. I recognize that when I release my need to hurry this party along, to orchestrate the menu and time every course, I actually enjoy the meal more from an expectant guest's point of view. A hungry, life-gulping acceptance.

It'll be delicious—His peace and rest offerings—even if dessert is delivered in an ER waiting room.

3
LOSS IS MORE

An Invitation to Hope in the Midst of Pain

Better to give up my quest for control and live in hope.
— Jerry Sittser, *A Grace Disguised*

Dear Dad,

You're supposed to be alive. Throwing the boys on the couch with your silly game of "I am the King!"; sending goofy texts; ushering Mom to the car for a drive south to zip along the coast and stop at El Ranchito, sharing carnitas with extra guacamole and a large Coke. You're supposed to be heaving your shoulders in guttural laughs and giving "pat-pat" hugs. You're supposed to be falling asleep horizontally on the couch, us talking by the cozy fire, your right hand twirling the temple tips of your glasses like a silent noisemaker then settling at the corner of your mouth, as up and down it rises to the beat of subtle snores.

But you're not here, and three years later the pain doesn't go away. Yesterday at church, while singing "Great Are You, Lord," a man in the front aisle wore Sperry loafers, sported short gray hair, carried your build, and for a moment it was *you*. It was you, your hands cupped heavenward, and it took everything in me not to bolt down the aisle, hug him, and hold his face in hopes of finding yours.

Tears come along with that familiar volcano fire in my throat when I accept for the millionth time that you are.not.

here. And I both hate it and am forever altered by your death. It has been life changing from a perspective I didn't expect. In how I view faith. In how I experience God's Spirit in such personal, creative ways. In caring less about arriving and choosing to lean into the hope of eternity. In surrendering control and anticipating what's around the unknown bend. In enjoying the process. I know (wink)—how long did you encourage me to "enjoy the journey"? I finally am. You're welcome.

In accepting the uncomfortable symptoms of pain and loss and grief and sorrow, I find it's in the sacred middle where I am wholly dependent on actually needing Jesus in the first place to remind me there is more than this temporalness.

Loss has stilled me to value, not fear, suffering. For in your absence, I've come to understand the Jesus I always wanted to know but didn't need. Before loss I chose a one-way relationship where I kept Him at arm's length, close enough to call on but far enough to feel alone. Dad, your passing has ruined me in the best way possible. I've never been so alive. And I know all this explosive beauty and raw loss is meant to draw me to an eternal Father who meets in the tenderest corners of grief and makes new what seemed lost. Even so, I miss you every.single.minute.

Dad, do you remember telling me days before your stroke, "I just wish you guys didn't have to suffer"? There are inklings, wondering if you knew your time on earth was coming to a close. I'm curious if God was allowing a brief glimpse of what lay ahead to prime the pump for loss so that I could walk into it with my eyes and soul open to how it would change *every*— and I mean *every*—thing.

As I stepped into the pain of loss, into the foggy weeks of numbness and standing outside of my body, life shifted. They say pain does that, and it's entirely true. And freeing. Alone with my thoughts of loss, I recognized habits I'd developed to perform, encourage, give, serve, force an often exhausted Bekah to pour *more* or to surround myself with others.

Perhaps if I host more or work harder or make this person feel special, I'll feel better. The only bummer was I no longer cared. I was done fighting. I was done *willing* faith. I had all the right ingredients, but they were self-made and I was burnt out.

As I sat outside, my legs folded under our weathered bench, for the first time, I *was*. I didn't *do*. I simply existed.

I'm done, God. I'm tired. I have nothing to give to anyone. Especially You. These feeble confessions changed my perspective on faith. For the first time, I let go of all the people-pleaser, perfectionist goals, the to-do lists and playdates, and the faces I hoped to make happy, and I got real down and dirty with my Lord. Getting real with Him saved my life. It drew me into deep layers I hadn't known existed. Into uncomfortable, foreign corners I fought all my life. Always present, He walked ahead, His hand near, His light illuminating the step needed for that moment, to say, *"I've heard you say you want to know Me all your life. Well, here I am. I will make something new from this pain, and it will be beautiful. Will you trust Me?"*

Do you remember me telling you, "Dad, I just want to hear God's voice? I want all this church stuff to mean something in real life"?

Bam.

Now it does.

Before losing you to an unexpected stroke, I didn't imagine loss as part of my ideal life plan. *Umm. No. I'd like to avoid suffering at all costs, please. Only fun parties are on the agenda.* Reality hits. Lava burns my throat, and tears fall hot. Guess what your death did to my precious, controlling life plan? It messed all that up. But God. He used loss as the catalyst for hope beyond this, to cut through the crowd's buzz, to focus on details, to usher me toward noticing faces through the masses, to worry less about the extra, and to crave genuine beauty waiting to be praised today.

Loss, Dad, *is* more. It provides a narrowed, stripped-down, beauty-from-ashes, life-from-death perspective. It takes the future I intended, turns it upside down, shakes my goals, and replaces them with Real's plan. Loss pulls away cobwebs from my eyes and clears a dull humming in my ears, and forces me to evaluate what really matters.

Loss transforms. Puts aside the fluff. Bends low to an essential Jesus. Loss replaces the whir of busy and places a funnel to listen to a God I've always wanted to hear. A Savior I've always wanted to know. A relationship I heard others talk of and knew was possible but, until suffering was upon me, didn't depend on for my next breath.

Loss *is* more.

Loss pulls out the shadowed colors and brings them to vivid light. It focuses a flashlight on the present, and for that moment, the present is all to be celebrated and grabbed on to, for beyond the brilliant light is He who holds eternity. And for this reason, suffering is stomached, not because it's easy to swallow but for the sheer joy at knowing life waits on the other side.

During the initial days of numb loss, where I felt like a raw nerve ending walking around on high alert and sensitivity (*bzzzz, bzzzz*), I noticed how God does indeed make all things new from suffering, my recent awareness coming from Tanner's preschool director. At pickup, where I arrived in sweats and glazed in a throbbing grief fog, Marge eyed me. Her neck cocked and eyes narrowed. She smiled intently. "You're different," she pointed out. "You've trimmed the fat."

I don't know how she noticed, but God knew I needed those words. They've stayed with me every day after. Your loss, Dad, trimmed the fat. It cleared away the extra and focused sharply and gently on *who* and *what* are important. I realized this when I thought back to the hospital week where you lay in a coma, after we received word that your stroke was actually kidney cancer metastasized to your brain and that you were terminal. "Months, if not weeks, to live," the doctor said. Odd how quickly our prayer went from hoping you'd wake up to releasing you, as Mom said, "to the One who loves you fully and completely." During that week, I didn't think about myself once.

Before, I was concerned with my schedule, my worries, often escaping the reality to ponder when my life would actually start happening. A tiny miracle happened in that hospital with you. I was so present to your situation that selfish distractions weren't a priority. That's the beauty of loss, of cutting the fat. It's having sharp eyes to see how, from death, comes life. Responding to losing you shifted my perspective toward a God who brings hope, where before I hoped to escape the average mundane details of today. C. S. Lewis wrote, "Pain insists upon being attended to. God whispers to us in our pleasures, speaks in our consciences, but shouts in our pains. It is his megaphone to rouse a deaf world."[7] Losing you roused me from a deaf, selfish world.

Suddenly life has purpose. Beauty in cracks. I can't stare at Tanner's freckles long enough or breathe in Ty's hair, smelling of burnt brown sugar, or want more than anything to be near Bryan, his arm around my neck like a safety scarf. I am voracious for today, however it's offered, and I don't want to miss a moment, for I know in this moment is where God breaks through to know and be known, and even if it's in pain, I choose to "give it my full attention so that it can teach me what I need to know about the Really Real."[8]

Simplistic awareness is what Jerry Sittser experienced when he lost his wife, his four-year-old daughter, and his mother in a horrific car accident and shared about in his inspiring book, *A Grace Disguised*. "Deep sorrow often has the effect of stripping life of pretense, vanity and waste. It forces us to ask basic questions about what is most important in life. Suffering can lead to a simpler life, less cluttered with nonessentials. It is wonderfully clarifying. That is why many people who suffer sudden and severe loss often become different people."[9] When I read his last line, my heart connected to his understanding of loss. I am different now. Focused. The fat trimmed. With an attuned *loss-is-more* heartbeat.

Months after you died, my friend Ingrid walked my same steps and called from the hospital room in Sweden where her father was dying. "Don't hold back," I told her. "Tell him you love him and why. What he means to you. Ask for forgiveness and offer it in return. Share and listen and savor this time with him now." As a daughter grieving my own father, I found a shared joy in gifting her these words. I imagined her hunched close to her dad's bed, similar to how I did with you, while outside his hospital window, a Swedish sky turned dark. It was an honor to exchange a flurry of texts, a phone call with a kindred soul across the ocean, one who was stepping onto an unpaved grief road. She told me later that her dad asked her to call certain people to share his love and thanks for them.

Ingrid said, "My faith and hope and heart and capacity for love have all changed from seeing my dad take his last breath."

Dad, did you see from heaven's balcony how your loss changed me from the inside out? Did you observe my interactions? Did you witness leaky, hot tears on my pillow? Did you watch as I walked into the kitchen countless times only to ask aloud, "What am I doing?" Did you count how often Tanner asked, "Are you crying? Do you miss Papa?" then whispered into my neck, "Me, too"? Did you lean closer to earth when Ty shared about a dream you were in or asked what heaven is like? Did you hear the churning of my stomach? Note my awareness at details obstructed before?

Are you aware that everyday conversations fiercely offered another side of "Who's coming for dinner?" "How was work?" "Wanna play Legos?" to clutching my heart and wondering aloud, "Dad, what are you doing in heaven? The boys miss you. Tanner confesses wondering if God is real because he can't see Him. Dad, why aren't you here to take him for yogurt and offer your heaven perspective? Why don't you tell him God is not a taker but a giver and, in relating to us in our suffering, is the most real a relationship can be? Compassion is the extreme side of love, the boldest, purest suffering salve.

"How close, Dad, do you stand to God? In His omnipotence, is He all-surrounding and therefore near you at all moments? If so, during the first months after you died, did you hear me talk to you first, and then Him as an afterthought? You were my misguided landline to God."

Then one night my whispers shifted from you to Jesus. Sleep hasn't been the same since you've been gone, and when slumber evaded and black minutes turned to hours, over and over I breathed, *Jesus, Jesus, Jesus.* His name was often the first and last word on my tongue, not out of holy reverence but for no other reason than I couldn't find another word. Even without looking for Him, He found me. In the dark. Tired. Blank. Sad. And He offered His comfort.

Dad, I know His voice now. I'm experiencing His Spirit as I pack lunches, power walk around the duck-filled lake bed, hug Anna, our Peruvian neighbor, and chat about how big the boys are getting. I'm in constant relationship with our Creator. Your death was the catalyst, and I can't imagine going back to how I lived before.

Before your death, I thought of heaven, in all honesty, as boring. How sad but true. And that's growing up in the church. Cue singing angels and fluffy clouds and hymns. Oh, *and* God. He was the bonus to an eternity of hanging out together. Loss and pain are teaching me that *believing* is the essence of what I hold to as a *believer*. I'm coming to understand the definition of *heaven* when I read in scripture about earth being a shadow of what's to come.

Simple enjoyments like honeymoon Fridays, tropical passion tea lattes, smooching our sons ("Mom, stop!"), chocolate macaroon pie, and getting lost in awe of ocean waves are a tease for more. And I've always wanted more. *The shiniest version of more.* But now it's not about what I'm going to get out of heaven—it's about opting to see it from the underbelly of suffering. For in aching and missing you like crazy, I've come to value and need hope. Stripped-down, focused, straight-to-the-heart-of-real-life hope. For it's better, as author Barbara Brown Taylor encouraged, "to go where the pain leads, down to the ground floor where all the real things are: real love, real sorrow, real thanks, real fear."[10] When we opt to find faith through life's unpredictable steps, we discover Jesus at Real's core.

No one wants to lose people, but I've experienced riches beyond this world in God's Spirit of comfort—of scattering heart-shaped leaves on the park path, painting love in the sky, whispering, *"Look up and down and around. Notice how My hope is ever present and inviting you to experience a wee bit of eternity here, confetti of the party I'm planning in heaven."*

Dad, remember Lindsay? When she looks back at her first marriage, a swirl of mansions and status and a ring bigger than our cottage, she realizes the god she worshipped was money. Weeks after they returned home from their honeymoon, she found a questionable e-mail leading to her new husband's affair. Yes, I know you would've punched the fellow. After their annulment, she was left in the wake of a failed marriage with questions like: "Where in the world is hope in a shattered marriage?" I remember her telling me about how she would literally get on her knees and beg God's Spirit to show up. She was at rock bottom, and no ring or beach house could fill the loss of being cheated on. But it was in her heartbreak that her faith was reignited. Pain is the most unchosen catalyst to an authentic faith journey.

She's an entirely new person now, Dad. She looks the same, but she shines with a knowing confidence. She has the trust of someone who stared loss in the face and boldly told it she would not be swallowed up by despair but would flourish in spite of hardship. Her story, one of letting God carry her through her brokenness, brought her to Steve, and years later, babies, and a life she never intended, and now can't imagine writing a more transformed ending. She.knows.hope.

Dad, there are epic losses and everyday losses, like when kids get sick and spouses come home stressed after a long day at work. A friend comes to mind, one who experienced an unexpected loss in the form of a panic attack in the middle of a church service, the same church she'd attended for twenty years. As she got curious about her body's reaction, she admitted she didn't feel like she fit into the community she'd been doing life with for so many years. "I was trying so hard to be a part of, to be valued, to earn the approval of a group of friends." One day it hit her. "I felt like an old salt and pepper shaker in a lovely china cabinet." By responding to her body's plea for deeper connection, she went to counseling and did the hard work to discover more about herself, prayed about the kind of friend she wants to be, and sought the type of life-giving relationships she deserves. Stepping out in faith, she walked into a new church community, where God is meeting her in authentic ways, walking alongside her, healing the pain of not "fitting in," and transforming her new friendships into an experience of wholeness and acceptance, even in all her salt and pepper shaker glory.

When flower centerpieces wither and die days after a party, we can use the fallen petals and, like death, repurpose them into something new. Although a different, unexpected new, this purpose still has beauty. Do you notice, Dad, how God does the same? He arranges the fallen petals in our lives to confetti a tablescape for everyday settings, where they hint at memories of what *was* and offer hope for what can *be*.

Loss can come from a stroke caused by cancer. From broken marriages and shattered hearts. From ER visits and anxiety attacks. From desperately trying to conceive or from mourning a lost babe. But gosh, Dad, there are also Cheerio-sized losses happening daily to people desperately wanting to know how God is real.

There's loss when we argue with our spouse about the dinner menu, when really it's not about the dinner menu but about years of hurt churning below the surface.

A friend finds two nails in her van tires. *Loss.*

Another despises her mirrored reflection. *Loss.*

A mom is at her wits' end, giving parenting everything she has and feeling a failure. *Loss.*

The Internet is down, the sale is over, the house is a mess. *Loss.*

A friend confesses, "He's not like the man I once married." *Loss.*

We spill spaghetti sauce on the floor. *Loss.*

A rat invades the garage and eats a hole in the washing machine hose. *Loss.*

Friendships shift. *Loss.*

There's the loss of a dream or a job or dismissed opinions. The loss of what could be. The loss of what is.

With every loss comes the choice to say, *God, help me experience You in this.* No matter how painful or heart wrenching, help me glimpse how dried flower petals hint of a past party *and* a purposeful future.

Dad, the initial weeks after you were gone, Mom and I busied ourselves in crowds. Walking into stores, touching soft dresses, and smelling fragrant candles. Distracting our pain in crowds felt good, as though we were attending a giant party but didn't know the other guests. This party had shapes and lights and colors, but some were more clearly in focus than others. Suffering does that. It awakens the soul and pushes PLAY on noticing, on being curious, on emphasizing everyday details once rushed by, now to be gobbled up with appreciation and reverence. Suddenly storefront signs, sounds of kids laughing, the spraying of fountains as we pass Nordy's E-Bar, and the smell of ground coffee beans stir me to experience God in real time. Right now. *Why hadn't I experienced this before?* It's as if I'd lived in black and white, and now suddenly I'm living my life, although painfully sad, in palpable color. Colors emulating sunflowers, peonies, and rose petals.

Colors. Dad, they've become God's personal gift in grief. The shiny red Coca-Cola truck whizzing by, the vibrant magenta rose opening her smiling face to the sun, the dismal gray and sterile white hospital floor underneath the bed you lay on for seven days after your stroke. All of these colors make up paint used to sweep the sky. In my imagination, grief was the shade of stormy charcoal clouds hovering above sad heads—gray and nothing colored, but what I'm actually discovering is that inside and around and shining through the pasty grief pouf are dazzling majestic colors too radiant to put into words. They sparkle and glow in the most unexpected ways. For where there is loss, hope also abounds.

From my desk, I look out the window where a wine barrel embraces a gift in your honor. A David Austin rose, like one of the dozens in your backyard, brings memories of you and Mom working side by side on Saturday mornings, pruning and trimming, Li'l Mom creating bouquets for neighbors and dropping them off to friends. David Austins, though. They are special. More fragrant than an average rose, with a cabbage-like bloom. Your favorite. Now my favorite. A smile comes quickly as I note a surprise on the William Shakespeare rosebush, which smells heavenly. It was a gift from the girls at my nurture table, the friends I bonded with over parenting challenges, questions, and doubts. Our hearts connected over learning and growing and now grieving together. They flooded our living room days after you passed and sat with me in silence. Some shared stories. Some asked. But mostly they came to say, *We love you. We hurt with you. And we have something to remind you there is hope even in loss. There is life in death.* They led me outside to this wine barrel where I buried my face and saw you smiling behind my eyelids.

Pressing my cheek to the glass, I glimpse a tiny bud opening her petals heavenward. Toward the Son. And the passage Netti shared, Numbers 6:24–26, her arm around mine and my hand clutching yours under fluorescent hospital lights, floods my soul: "The LORD bless you and keep you; the LORD make his face shine on you and be gracious to you; the LORD turn his face toward you and give you peace."

His face, Dad. I can feel His warmth on mine even when I'm not in the sun.

When God manifests through loss to offer grief healing, friends who understand, a redeemed marriage, or a safe community, hope is conceived. Dad, perhaps the Divine collects a myriad of shades from each flower as varnish to color the world.

Karen, who you referred to as "one of your daughters," texted me the morning after you passed: I CAN'T HELP BUT WONDER IF GOD LETS THE NEWCOMERS PAINT THE SUNRISE.

And I'm so glad you chose the deep crimson hue of David Austin's William Shakespeare bloom.

I love you, Dad.

Until eternity,

Bekah Jane

WHO AM I?

An Invitation to Claim a Jesus Identity during Transition

Light precedes every transition. Whether at the end of a tunnel, through a crack in the door or the flash of an idea, it is always there, heralding a new beginning.
—Teresa Tsalaky, *The Transition Witness*

J'll never forget an outdoor winery wedding I coordinated where the DJ was awful. Just awful, bless his heart. His job was to keep the schedule flowing and guests entertained. Preferably with tunes sung by Justin Timberlake, Adele, or Bob Marley. All night I held his hand. Prompting. Directing. Keeping him on track. "Okay, now it's time to excuse guests to eat." "Now gather everyone for cake cutting." "Where is your run sheet?" "No, I don't want to emcee. . . Okay, fine." At one point, I think I grabbed the mic and announced the garter toss. The saving grace? A doughnut bar. Bless those tiger tails. I even shared some with the guests.

Like music at a wedding, life details seamlessly transition from one to the next. Until they don't. Have you ever been on the dance floor, rocking sweet moves next to the bride and groom, when the dreaded occurs? *Whatever happens, please don't stop the music* (fist bump, Rhianna). If you've lived long enough, you know this moment all too well. The DJ takes a break. Or the singing stops. Or the playlist quits. In the quiet space, guests look around and wonder, *What happened so unexpectedly? Where's the music? Is something wrong?*

Isn't it funny how we go merrily on our way until a shift occurs, and then we panic? *I knew this was coming, but really? Why isn't this going as planned? Where is God in this transition?*

What if it's possible not to be thrown by transition—where life was before, where we believe it ought to go—but to respond to it with trusting faith by clinging even tighter to a constant God. In his book *Yes or No*, Jeff Shinabarger echoes how transition urges us to seek Real. "Moments of transition often lead us to the knowledge of our own limits and the recognition that we need help from beyond ourselves."[11] Since transitions are the symptoms of ever-changing life, how we respond to them reveals our true identity.

So what *is* identity? It's who you *are*. What your value and worth depend on. Or better yet, *whose* you are. Identity is at the core of the story God is writing in your unique life.

Years of event managing rooted an identity crisis in me, one our culture plays on repeat: life must be lived from one event to the next with an epic, nonstop playlist cheering every circumstance. The danger of *ideal*. Maybe some Bob Marley swaying, salt-air-in-the-hair, carefree, never-ending tunes. Reality: an event lasts maybe a day, but the majority of life is lived in the lull, the in-between moments until the next party occurs. If a conductor such as Gustav Mahler knows that "the real art of conducting consists of transitions," we as music listeners recognize the same truth.[12]

And the truth is? The music *will* stop. The band *will* take a break. The singing *will* give way to instruments then silence. Transition *will* come, and with it a choice to run ideals, emotions, and roles through our identity filters.

Does this mean the party is a *flop*? Or is it an opportunity to look deeper and discover an unchanging faith when outside songs can't be heard?

I believe there is something brave and noble and exciting about transition and all possibilities surrounding it. There's also something petrifying and disappointing and mundane in the midst of transition. It's known as reality, and for years it shook my identity and pulled honest utterings of "Who am I?" Wobbly and unsure when circumstances shifted—some intentionally and others completely unforeseen—I admittedly noted how similar life proved to be as it was before, but doing the same thing in a unique place.

Like many of you, my first transition rodeo was college. "Training ground for transition" every college application should read. Azusa Pacific University–bound, the idea of moving (*cough*) a mere thirty minutes away fueled my inner optimist. I was eager for *new* friends, *new* classes, *new* surroundings. You recognize the theme song? *New* must be *better*. Surely, change will offer a brighter version of my current *not-so-new* life. Thus the downside, the underbelly of ideal: striving for a standard of perfection in the next.big.change.

Aaand guess what happened? A month after scaring my poor Midwest roommate with just so, *so* many words, saying yes to every social engagement/Bible study/extracurricular opportunity/study group/midnight brownie-eating extravaganza, and telling myself I was settling into the freshman routine, the newness was now *old*. I wasn't prepared for confusion at why I felt let down after coming off the high of change chasing, but I am thankful. It led me to ask honest questions and fight to experience faith found in reality rather than ideals.

Who are my people? What do I seriously want to do with the rest of my life? What does this guy think about us hanging out? Are we dating? Should I be dating? I don't even have time for a man.

And the ever-constant question: *Who am I?*

It's safe to say whenever life gets shaky, a wrench thrown in my fabulously intended plans, an identity crisis is triggered and I have to examine one of these areas: ideals, emotions, or roles.

Ideals. As an optimist, the fun side shines when dreaming of the potential for any person or situation. The downside, though, elevates my expectation beyond reach, wraps it in a perfect package, then guarantees I will no doubt be disappointed when I realize it is not a standard that can be met.

Emotions. You know, those feelings we get about circumstances, especially those surrounding change? Get in touch with them. Pay attention. We have them for a reason. Don't ignore them. Be curious about your emotions.

Roles. Better known as what we do. Our jobs. How we spend our hours. A label or title we go by. Currently, I'm writing on my couch, so you could say my new role is couch potato. (If only cookie dough was within reach.)

Since much wisdom can be found in books written for little munchers, I connect to the literary genius Mo Willems (it may have to do with his hilarious illustrations, too) as he expresses all three of these identity nudges in one read. (Thank you, Mo. May I please be a character in your next series?)

His children's book *My New Friend Is So Fun* is about two best friends, Piggie and Elephant. Piggie makes a new friend, Bryan the Bat, and spends lots of time with him. But Elephant begins to panic, telling Snake, "They could be having more fun than they have with us!" So, Elephant draws the conclusion that maybe Piggie doesn't need him anymore. He decides to put an end to all the fun Piggie and Bat are having. When Elephant and Snake approach Piggie and Bat, they learn the news that, yes, they are having a lot of fun. They are even making best friend drawings. Elephant nearly has a meltdown, shouting, "It is worse than I feared!" Piggie proudly holds up her "Best Friend Drawing," a picture of Elephant, while Bat shows a drawing of Snake. "You made drawings of—US!" they ask incredulously. "Of course," says Piggie. "You are our best friends," smiles Bat.[13]

What makes this endearing story so relatable to young children and seasoned souls is how it resonates with our identity in regard to

Ideals: Piggie and Elephant are best friends and always will be.

Emotions: Elephant is insecure and worries that Bat is more fun than he is and maybe Piggie won't need him.

Roles: Elephant freaks out and tries to stop Piggie from having "too much fun" because his role as best friend is threatened. What he learns, however, is his identity is in safe standing with Piggie. Even when they are apart, Elephant isn't missing out. But he has to trust their relationship in order to experience peace.

So. Been. There.

How I wish I would have known that when transition happens, it's scattered with a gamut of emotions from one end of the spectrum to the other. Starting is the exciting *ideal*, but it's the journey through the middle where faith and identity are refined. Isn't it easy to assume that if we're embracing change, what follows will be easy? But it's the messiness of transition, the center, that builds dependence on Jesus and roots a solid identity. What if we don't have to look back? What if we can have a confident Christ identity, knowing He is enough in the here and now?

If it's hard, you're on the right track. Because recognizing the hard, my friend, is necessary to actually needing a Savior, and that Savior *cannot be you*.

My college years signaled awareness inklings of my need for Real. Experienced in fast-forward beats, I knew little of how to offer myself permission to look for faith invitations. I was downright panicked at the thought of stilling myself long enough to plant my feet in who I was when no one else was around and grow comfortable with God's voice. The problem was I didn't need Him. Not just yet.

Marriage brought its own transition. "How come you want to sit and veg out after work? Don't you want to talk about your day and hold hands on a walk?" *Who am I without my spouse?* I wondered.

It wasn't until we made a brave, much prayed-over move from Orange County, California, four hours north to a town in the central coast, where the population is still more cows than humans and the biggest deal is a Target two cities north, that starting over became scary. We're talking major transition, people. Big changes. Exciting. Petrifying. But if you are a planner, a doer, a "let's get this party started" personality, you'll understand that leaping toward transition isn't the challenge; it's what happens in the middle. After we set up our new kitchen, my husband enjoyed a hearty laugh, pulling back cardboard flaps, discovering *tins* upon *boxes* of tea. "Really, you need that much tea?" he asked. "Yes, if the apocalypse occurs, bring your kettle. I have English Breakfast."

Once unpacked, the quiet invaded, and I sat on our couch,

which was stuffed against our tiny cottage wall, and sighed. *Now what? Why did God bring us here? Where are our people? Who do I call to go antiquing? Where do I get my hair done?* This was my first invitation to transition my temporary identity found in people to a permanent identity secure in Jesus. It was here uncomfortable symptoms of transition surfaced; I was no longer in my control. I had no community to run to. No shops to fill my time with. Heaven forbid I went on Sunday; they were closed. *Welcome, Laura Ingalls.*

So you know what I did? I thought about going into a deep, dark depression. I figured, *This is it. This is what it feels like when I'm not okay. When I don't have the answers. When God isn't showing up with His part of the plan. This party isn't full of merry tunes and catchy beats. Why isn't confetti raining from the sky? We did listen to His voice with this move, right? (Frantically turning my head in every direction.)*

But here's the thing: I wasn't equipped with enough life experiences to know that God longs to meet me in my conflicting emotions. When life is hard, it doesn't necessarily mean I am depressed. When life is hard, it means I have a choice. I can press into the uncomfortable arenas change brings and experience Him in them, or I can fill them with busyness, people, work, whatever. When I read *Yes or No*, I laughed at the truth of Jeff Shinabarger's thoughts. "Why is it that, as a culture, the minute we lose a job or are in some kind of transition, the question we ask each other is this: What are you going to do next? This is an unhealthy pressure to put on one another. . . . Transition times give us the opportunity to step back and ponder our purpose."[14] I'd like to say I allowed myself to be uncomfortable. To be terrified and lonely and acknowledge God's care in that tiny house that backed up to the riverbed, which backed up to our new church, which welcomed our new community, which scared the heck out of me. But I refused to appreciate the pause, the lull, the necessary sonnets carried by lament. Deep down I craved God's voice, His safe presence in foreign surroundings. I heard Him calling when I lay on our denim couch and cried buckets of tears. "I'm not okay," I told Bryan. But really, what is being okay? What's the definition? Have you asked yourself the same question when life doesn't go as planned? Does being okay mean comfortable? Happy? Having this current circumstance dialed in? And if I'm willing to continue digging deeper and being vulnerable, I assumed being okay meant I wasn't scared. Or disappointed. Or panicking about our decision to move because the surroundings weren't wedding music–like, fun and celebratory.

Transition triggered every intolerable, untapped emotion inside and pulled out a variety of feelings I wasn't familiar with—anger, fear, frustration—and offered them on a platter. Before, the only feelings I knew of were extremes on the emotion spectrum—joy or depression. It must be one or the other, right?

Emotions, however, are like notes to a song—there are many, and they rise and fall. When I'm transparent about my emotions, even when they scare me and I notice discomfort, my natural reaction is to push them away, to get over them, and live in the ideal, a magnifying glass on the best version of the current circumstance. Emotions are not my identity, but God uses them.

Jesus, I'm learning, is near me in emotions. He says, *"I relate. I get it. And as much as you are sad or unsettled, I, too, have felt that way, and I am bigger than your feelings."* And then He encourages me to depend on Him when I want to lead with my emotions. As God said in Joshua 1:9, "Have I not commanded you? Be strong and courageous. Do not be afraid; do not be discouraged, for the LORD your God will be with you wherever you go." Feelings hint at my very need to cling closer to the Father, who created them. He fills in the gaps between my independence and dependence, completing my worth in Him.

If you're in a place of transition, please know that you are not alone. It's the bravest and scariest place to be because you can't control the aftermath of how this change will affect you. What I'm learning about transitions really comes down to a choice: Will I step into the song playing when the uncomfortable feelings rise to the surface? When frustration and fear and downright panic emerge because this unfamiliar score seems wobbly, will I peer past my circumstances and believe faith is built with one shaky dance step forward? Or will I sing lines I've forever sung, of being in charge, depending on myself to orchestrate and make the music happen?

During those first epic transitions, I initially skipped down the comfy path, banking on sheer willpower and a smile stitched across my face. I postponed my Maker's offer; I pushed away His nearness because I thought meeting Him on the mountaintop was where real faith was experienced. I never sat in the discomfort long enough to recognize His closeness, to understand how He was offering a genuine relationship, one in which He was totally okay sitting in the discomfort with me. Faith isn't moving past the fear; faith tolerates the tension and relaxes into His compassionate comfort.

Eagerness for the next event overshadowed the reality of mundane days between. Then I beat myself up for feeling disappointed when it didn't live up to the idea I'd created in my imagination. This was supposed to be fun and life changing. The problem was I forgot that when life changed, the life-changing reality, the transition, wasn't always easy.

When we had our first son, the music came to a sudden stop. Not even classical Baby Einstein playing in the background. Nuh-uh. Nothin'. Screeching halt, friends. Cue identity crisis. Suddenly I was staring at this striped onesie–donned babe, covered in spit-up, and familiar words erupted from within: *Who am I?* Yes, I can be a stubbornly slow learner. There I went again, mistaking my daily roles for my identity as a Jesus follower. Feed. Change. Dress. Wipe poop off the sweatshirt I'd worn three days in a row. Dream of planning events and putting on lip gloss and creating with a team of adults.

Roles, however, don't dictate my identity. I took pride in my former career as an event planner and judged those who were self-admitted "worriers." *Why worry when you can plan?* I thought. Planner, I found, was a fancy title for Worrier, for if the plan didn't stay with the agenda, self-doubt rooted. And self-doubt can only root if I believe that's where my worth comes from. When I read about worry in Matthew 6, about how God cares for birds and lilies dressed more exquisitely than Solomon, about how He asks, "Can any one of you by worrying add a single hour to your life?" (verse 27), I used to judge and laugh and shake my head. But holy smoke, that's what I was doing, only I justified it because I was a planner. If schedules went haywire, my anxiety level skyrocketed into fix-it mode, relying on brazen efforts to make the agenda happen. Too often I fought the transition instead of responding to what God was trying to teach me through it.

When I've shared about how hard being a new mom was,

other mamas have come out of the woodwork, and I realize we are not alone, us planner moms. Struggling to find purpose after welcoming babies is a real thing. I think of a close friend who directed a senior care facility, leading a team and meeting goals, sitting behind a large desk and bringing home a weighty paycheck. Now she has two munchers, three and under, and it has been a difficult transition for her. She admits feeling like the same song is playing on REPEAT day after day. Her temptation is to idealize her career, entertaining thoughts of feeling more valuable if she returns to that job. But as she listens to what's really playing in her head and heart, she recognizes a familiar tune: discontentment. The same notes that played even when she led a successful career and lived a luxurious life in a La Jolla beach house. Even now with sweet babes underfoot, she knows God wants to refine her identity. She admits her desire, like Paul wrote about in Philippians 4:11, "to be content whatever the circumstances."

As years continue, the scenery and songs, they change.

Fill in your own blank. What responsibilities and circumstances consume the majority of your hours these days? Sitting at a desk? Caring for an aging parent? Finishing that paper before the sun comes up? Staring at your bestie, a.k.a. your washing machine, churning tiny onesies and socks you will never find again?

Those duties, my dear friend, are not *who* you are. They are everyday tasks begging to be accomplished. And in a few years, they will change and a new mantle will settle, and with it, perhaps a bigger paycheck or more stability or greater freedom or different questions, and you'll notice that familiar phrase return like the quiet interchange before the next song plays.

Who am I?

My groundbreaking decision came in declaring, I'm not *just* a mom. I'm also not *just* a wife or a friend or a daughter or an obsessive-compulsive furniture rearranger or cookie dough binger. I'm not just a writer or a storyteller or a curly haired speed walker.

As Lindsay so beautifully truth bombed via text: You are a daughter of the King (I mean really, you don't need anything else). You are smart, talented, beautiful inside and out, anointed, wise, funny, so fun, a bomb baker, bestest friend, driven, inspiring, eloquent, sassy, and all around amazing. The end.

And Jesus echoes the same.

We are made in His image. (Genesis 1:26–27)
Fearfully and wonderfully made, that is. (Psalm 139:14)
We are chosen. (1 Peter 2:9)
We are the dwelling space for the Holy Spirit.
    (1 Corinthians 6:19–20)
He loves us even when we mess up. (1 Corinthians 13)
Simply because He is our Father and we are His
    children. (1 John 3:1)

This is where we find our identity. This is who.we.are. When situations shift, I care less about trying to force authenticity and more about simply depending on a genuine Jesus. When I do, my focus naturally transfers from *me* to *Him*.

Is that enough? Is claiming a Jesus identity that fits as snug and cozy as your comfy pants enough?

Now when moves, career changes, babies, or serious illnesses come, I find comfort knowing I am *enough*, for the

Spirit of the Lord lives inside me. No matter what happens, my identity will not be shaken. This doesn't mean I don't get scared or disappointed or binge on obscene amounts of sea salt chocolate when Plan A is chiseled down to Plan Q; it just means I get another opportunity to walk outside, look into the night sky, and listen as trees rustle their created music. I recognize the tune carried and believe, "Whatever my lot, Thou hast taught me to say, 'It is well, it is well with my soul.'" When seasons shift, as Ecclesiastes 3:11 assures, He will make everything beautiful in its time. My prayer for myself, and I'll pray this for you as well, is that you will be rooted in God's truth, knowing that your ultimate value and worth are found in Him. As you live out of this truth, your identity will overflow into all you do and say, reflecting your Maker. May you know confidence and security when jobs, zip codes, and communities change. When your spouse doesn't get you, or your purpose seems foggy, or your kids are going nuts, remember *whose* you are. When you release control and allow Him to be enough, freedom comes—freedom to be present to His work in every detail of your life, trusting He is making all things new.

Even in transition.

5
UNDIE THERAPY

An Invitation to Beauty and Worth When You Feel Anything but Beautiful and Worthy

The most beautiful people we have known are those who have known defeat, known suffering, known struggles, known loss, and found their way out of the depths These persons have an appreciation, a sensitivity, and an understanding of life that fills them with compassion, gentleness, and a deep loving concern. Beautiful people do not just happen.

—Elisabeth Kübler-Ross

*P*lease imagine you're strolling the Target beauty aisle for shampoo and razors and notice a woman crouched low. She's dressed, uh. . .well, let's just say she's *maintaining*. Her hair? A hive of curly tangles. Her eyes? Puffy and vacant. Forget makeup. She's running her pointer finger along the fine print on every acne regimen in the facial products section. You peer closer and see she's crying. That woman, my friends, is yours truly. Because rocking this grief trip is already a blast, why not throw in my body wanting to join the party in the form of a breakout trail starting at my forehead and leading to my back? I'm a lovely hot mess. And surely one of these acne foam bottles is my saving grace.

If you bent eye level or touched my shoulder with a caring hand, I most assuredly would collapse on you in heaping sobs. *I feel so ugly. My dad just died, and everything is a fog. A weird focused fog, and* (I'd gesture to my appearance) *really I'm just surviving. And this?* (I draw your attention to my face.) *Do you see them? And here?* You look around at this point, unsure what to do with the crazy lady in the face wash aisle. You came to buy lotion and maybe snag that taupe nail polish on sale. My apologies. You are now a part of my grief-stricken zit abyss story. *And here.* (I gesture to my back.) *I even broke out on my back. How gross is that?* You're nodding. It is gross. Poor soul. She needs a padded cell and heavy-duty zit cream stat.

Will someone please tell me how, like *how* do our bodies get the memo before we do that stress—positive or negative stress—is occurring? Do they selfishly not want to miss out, so they decide to throw in headaches and carb cravings and breakouts, basically wreaking havoc on the outsides to meet our already havocked insides? Boo, stress. *Just boo.*

It doesn't fit the medical books, but my friend Gina gets pinkeye when she's stressed. In college she got it four or five times a year, always before a huge nursing midterm. Sweet soul. As if beginning studies at 2:00 a.m., surrounded by brownies and coffee, isn't challenging enough, she was forced to strain through gooey shades pulled down over sticky red eyes, occasionally prying a crusty eyelid from her eyeball in order to take notes on the handling of bodily fluids (is that a thing? Lord knows I'm no nurse).

Do you know this feeling? You break out before a big date, interview, or move. It happens like always, right? Stress in the form of zits or whatever it is your body does.

During fresh grief months, *beautiful* was not a word I would grab from thin air and proudly wear. I felt anything but beautiful. Small. Blemished. Ugly. Sad. Whittled down to the core, I felt exist-y. But beautiful? Far from it.

When my dad entered glory on April 2, I looked ahead at the calendar and decided to keep a speaking engagement at Atascadero Bible Church, the community where Bryan and I became us. We thought that maybe it would be good to go "home" for a weekend, to process as we drove through winding hills along the coastal 101 highway, away from distraction, without the boys. We would have time to talk about the sudden change and our new normal. And what better time to speak than in the middle of raw grief? There would be no putting a bow on this one, and I no longer wanted tidy bows. I wanted authentic *This is how God is meeting me right now. In grief. In ugliness. In joy.* These are the stories I wanted to hear, and these are the stories I will tell.

Spring in the central coast is on the cooler side, and I took advantage of long sleeves and high sweaters to hide red bumps on my chest and neck. My face was the problem. How could I speak when people would be distracted by flaming marks that no amount of makeup could cover up? Even so, I went.

I'm not sure if it was spotting the familiar profile of San Luis Obispo's emerald hills, or staying with our friends, the McDonalds, in their cozy red barn, or curling like bookends on the couch with Wendy as I poured out pain at missing my dad, but an unexpected sort of healing and being seen occurred that weekend. Wendy shared in the understanding of grief dynamics accompanying loss. She and her hubby, Stan, had lost their son, Clayton, two years earlier when he, their second child, released a lifetime battle with leukemia. For a season, Clayton was Bryan's middle school youth intern at the church, and I remember not knowing what to say when the leukemia came back and he opted for no more treatment.

The McDonald family knows grief, and they are beautifully changed by it.

I don't remember one word I shared at the retreat that weekend. What is forever etched in my memory is what happened on the way home. Crying on and off, because that was grief's lovely way of reminding me that the dad I've always known would not be waiting at home to greet us, we wound our way back along the 101, stopping in Santa Barbara. Santa Barbara, an ideal middle spot between Atascadero and Orange County, a pause for gas, coffee, stretching our legs to window shop our way to the pier, leaning over to breathe in salt air and stare at waves before driving the final hours home. We'd come to anticipate our Santa Barbara stops, especially eating at Pascucci's, an Italian gem with Chianti bottles, red candle votives, and killer lasagna.

A young college waitress led us to the back and seated us in a booth with a bench too low for the table. Looking across at Bryan, I felt like a small toddler, barely able to see him. A zitty, ugly, crying toddler. We ordered iced teas, and as sun filtered through a central skylight, we drank, but it felt robotic and void of taste. When the lasagna came, I reached for my fork, and they came. Heaving sobs. Thick, gulping, "I miss my dad; why won't this horrible movie stop?" sobs. My face hurt from crying. And every time I swiped at tears, my hand met hundreds of tiny, hard, burning blemishes, a reminder of not only how fragile I felt, but also how my ugly reflection mocked quivery insides. Bryan, unaffected by my outbursts, smiled and reached for my hand. Which only made me cry more.

"C'mon," he said, leaning over. "I've got something for you." I ate final bites by rote, washed them down with iced tea, and he practically carried me out of the restaurant, my hand tucked in his as he led the way toward El Paseo, a nook of stores I adore. "I don't feel like shopping," I said with a sigh. Friends, this is when you know grief is horrible.

"We're not shopping," he replied, smiling. "I'm taking you for undie therapy."

Okay, this is where I must tell you that while my husband is a romantic at heart, he is not a shopper. He seldom whisks me into stores and says, "Buy something. I'll sit here and watch you try on outfits by the hours." Nope. And *especially* lingerie stores. He'd rather die than enter a place selling underwear and bras and risk the chance of bumping into a student or mom from church. His face, no doubt, would match a stewed tomato, and I can only imagine the awkward scene that would unfold if he was caught holding lace hipsters for the entire world to witness. Nope, anytime he splurges on fun lingerie, it comes to our doorstep in a box. *Bless.*

Not that I blame him. Growing up, my mom's favorite perfume was Victoria's Secret, a clean romantic scent available in the back of the store, past the undies and bras and silk pj's. This was before they had separate shops for unmentionables and perfume, and my poor dad could not bring himself to walk inside. Call it embarrassment or too many life-size storefront visuals; it was not his comfort zone. Every Christmas Eve morning he'd wake me. "Bekah, get up. You have to come with me to Victoria's Secret so I can get Mom that perfume." First off, why he waited till the last hour is beyond me, but I'd pull back covers and throw on jeans and accompany him to the mall, where he'd hand me money and shift back and forth while I went inside to purchase "the biggest bottle they had" for Mom. It was endearing and sweet, and it became our inside joke, our Christmas Eve, Victoria's Secret tradition.

And here Bryan was offering undie therapy. His face was focused as he clutched my hand and pulled me forward, clearly a man on a mission. We entered the lingerie store, and he ushered me to bins of undies. "Pick some. Whatever you like." He reached into pink boxes and pulled out lace and satin underwear, bright pink and flowered ones. *He's gone mad*, I thought. *We have both gone officially mad.* When I recovered from the shock and understood he was serious, I joined the party, taking my time, strolling the store, running my fingers along soft fabrics, him *glued* to my side, and something internal brought me to tears. Except, for the first time in weeks, they were joy tears, sweet tears, brought on by his thoughtful gesture.

As I shopped, a full-length mirror caught my reflection. *This, my friends, is when it gets real.* Thick fluorescent beams (what is it about store lights?) illuminated dime-sized spotlights all over my blemished skin. I stood close to the mirror and detested my image. *Why did I have to look like a middle-aged teenager? Why did I have to feel so ugly in a season when I was already uncomfortable? And why were my chest and back covered in angry bumps?*

Bry's voice interrupted my thoughts. "Did you find any you like?" He turned me away from the mirror and cupped my face. And he spoke what I know now to be God's words through Bryan's mouth.

"I want you to know"—his eyes began filling—"that even though you don't feel beautiful right now, God wants me to tell you that you are. You are so beautiful. And even if nothing else seems that way, I want you to feel beautiful. That's why we're doing undie therapy." He held me under the intrusive light, and for that moment, I felt so unutterably seen and enough. Not in the physical sense, but of a quiet inner worth, knowing all the insecure pain would somehow ignite a different version of beauty from within.

I've never been so proud to walk out of a store on Bry's arm. Not for the reason that he proudly carried a small bag of gorgeous undies, but for what took place in the store. Later he shared that God gave him that idea, and not in a cheesy way but in a genuine, it-had-to-be-from-God-because-Bryan-would-never-set-foot-in-there way. And it spoke volumes to me. That afternoon in Santa Barbara, a sad girl was told she was beautiful, and she believed it.

God's Spirit was evident when He used Bryan to teach me to look deeper. To look past the facade and peer into the heart. When he took me for undie therapy, he offered a gesture rooting something eternal and sacred inside. "Beauty," as Plato said, truly "is in the eye of the beholder." As much as I didn't feel it, Bryan did, and in those first raw grief months, God used him to echo tangible worth reminders time and time again. In his words. In his safe arms to bawl. In the middle of having friends for dinner and excusing myself because it was all too overwhelming. He didn't waver once. He also didn't entirely get it. But he was God in the shape of my husband who offered the gift of undie therapy to meet a want I wasn't aware needed gentle tending.

In a way, we all need undie therapy in whatever form it comes. We all need God to use others to genuinely remind us that we are seen and found worthy and beautiful in their eyes and His. And you know who needs those reminders most? Not the beautiful people. I imagine they already hear those comments. You know who needs to hear, "You are absolutely beautiful"? Insecure teenagers and new parents and the teach-ers loving on kids day after day. Our neighbors and those in the fresh fog of loss ought to know they are unbelievably beautiful. We need to look into women's eyes—women who are fighting cancer, who are widows, who are exhausted from the rat race, who believe they need to look like the window dressings at the mall—and we need to point within and whis-per, "Beauty is only skin deep. But true beauty, that comes from the Father."

True beauty is letting God be strong when you feel done. Beauty is smiling even when your heart hurts. Beauty is trusting that your worth is solidified in a God of grace who knows your thoughts and fears and sees you giving your best today and wraps you in His embrace and shines a light on your face and declares, *"You. Are. Beautiful."*

I am honored to have met and know truly beautiful women. They shine because of their stories, not because of their dress size or perfect skin.

At Target (where else can you get bananas, tampons, and a cute top?) Ty spotted a bald woman in the band-aid section, and the following scene played out in slow motion. His eyes grew Frisbee-sized. His left hand out, pointer finger aimed, he stared at the woman's smooth head then grabbed Tanner and ran to the next aisle, where I heard him yell, "Did you see that lady? *SHE DOESN'T HAVE ANY HAIR!*"

Isn't parenting like eating humble pie till we feel we may burst?

I nonchalantly walked around the corner where our sons were speaking for all of Target to hear and met their eyes. "That woman in the aisle over," I explained, "has cancer, and she is so brave for rocking her beautiful, bald head. She doesn't have hair because the medicine she takes makes it fall out. Can you imagine how scary that must feel? What if instead of pointing and staring, we go tell her that she is beautiful?"

Tanner pushed Ty forward as the verbal sacrifice.

I watched our youngest approach her, and in a quiet voice, he squeaked, "I want to tell you that you are beautiful." The woman crouched low and smiled. "Thanks, sweetie."

I met her eyes and echoed the same. She is. She is by far one of the most beautiful women I've ever seen, and to this day, I don't remember her face, but I do remember her brave bald head and the courage it must have taken to walk out her front door and risk comments all day long like the ones my boys made.

When we arrived home, I called Donna, the mom of one of my dearest friends, Em; she's like a second mom to me. At the time, she was a three-year cancer survivor, and I told her what happened at the store and asked for advice. "What do I do if that happens again? What made you feel seen and valued when you went through chemo?" Donna shared about looking at her bald reflection for the first time. Once clumps of hair began falling out at work, she sped up the process and asked her son-in-law to shave her head. And then he shaved his own.

She shared about how she'd expected to cry. She didn't expect she'd *wince* every time her reflection stared back. "To this day, I still don't feel as pretty as I did before cancer. I had no idea how embarrassed or shy I would be or how I wouldn't even want my own husband to see my bald head. It was hard, constantly trying to hide my ugly from everyone."

Donna invited me deeper into her chemo experience, sharing vulnerable thoughts about what it was like being bald in public. She remembered people doing double takes and experiencing personal moments in front of the mirror, moments when she self-deprecated and believed the lie "I can only be beautiful with hair."

Donna encouraged me to invite a conversation with our kids about what's "behind the bald" when we see someone who is bald in public. Where so often we see only the physical symptoms of a serious illness, she offered another perspective. "Tell your kids that female baldness is likely a side effect of something else. If it's the result of a serious illness, there may be fear, anxiety, sadness, or hopelessness. Bald women may look around and see people who look better than they do and assume that those people are happy and without fear. Others don't care about the bald lady; they are just thankful not to be ugly. I was envious of that and felt desperate to feel normal again, not just physically but emotionally." Donna's advice to think about what's "behind the bald" helps me better understand how "chemo patients become slaves to a new normal of endless regular clinical procedures, big scary machines, routine and painful tests and trials. For years. Remember," Donna urges, "when you see a woman with a bald head, it could be and probably is so much more."

Donna inspires me to take the time to remind a cancer fighter how beautiful she is. "Without saying it, you're also telling them that you see them and you *know*. And you care." Her perspective on having cancer and redefining the term *beautiful* stilled my soul as she shared, "I believe that when God allows us to have cancer, He does so much to redeem it. He makes us brave to endure the road ahead. He makes us beautiful on the inside so it changes us and somehow makes us beautiful on the outside. He brings people that will tell us, in the grocery store or Target or at church or the mall. Next time you see someone bald and beautiful, tell her."

Beauty has nothing to do with skin, hairdos, or numbers on a scale. True beauty is when women choose to be authentically honest about their ugly experiences and, in doing so, become winsome.

I think of Jamie, a lifetime friend. Our moms met in a couples' Bible study before they had kids, and when they were both pregnant with us, our friendship was destined. Jamie recently had her first baby, a daughter named Nora. And before she had Nora, she and her husband, Doug, visited from Tennessee. We sat around our shabby kitchen table, and over messy tacos we asked how we could pray for them as they prepared to be parents.

What we weren't expecting was for Jamie's response to be so vulnerable. "You can pray for my body image," she confessed. "Having a history of abusing my body with overeating, binging, and overexercising, I want to be healthy for Nora, and"—she pointed at her belly—"being pregnant and gaining weight is not easy for me."

I just love it when people are transparent.

Jamie offered a window into her dark years of feeling unworthy. Before they married, she confided to Doug about her lifetime struggle with food addictions, and it was through Doug's intentional choice to marry her and stay by her side that she first experienced God's tangible love. "Whether you weigh 250 pounds or 80 pounds, I love you unconditionally. You are beautiful to me no matter what," Doug assured her. Do you know what his words did to Jamie's self-worth? They made her feel chosen. Aside from her parents, he was the first one to prove love, despite knowing her struggles with food and self-image. Even when she binged and felt horrible, didn't want to be touched, and pushed Doug away, he accepted her and told her she was stunning.

Participating in Overeaters Anonymous was another huge step toward Jamie's healing. Though she readily admitted her doubt that God actually cared about the little things like how fast she could inhale an entire large cheese pizza or how often she exercised, it was with her Overeaters Crew that she felt known. Understood. Worthy. She even noticed how she was hurting her husband when she projected critical and harsh words on Doug as a reflection of her own eating habits and claimed the phrase, "If you spot it, you got it," a flashlight shining on her own eating struggle. Understanding this made Jamie aware of how God saw her. When Nora joined their family, I adore how honestly she shared about her fear at having to eat more to care for a nursing baby. Suddenly I saw her body—the one she'd abused and despised—important not only in the receiving of love from her husband, but in the giving of life to her daughter, and when she told me, "With Doug, I understand in an earthly, tangible way a *fraction* of what it's like to receive God's unconditional love. With Nora, I understand how God gives unconditional acceptance, regardless of what we do to earn it. With Doug I received, and with Nora, I gave," I about lost it with ugly tears. I love how Jamie now respects her body and offers it back to her daughter with repurposed worth.

When Jamie talks with people struggling with eating disorders, I'm struck by how she chooses to respond to the beauty in everything, including the messy process. She admits that her addiction is not conquered, but that it is a "moment by moment choice." She says, "A food addiction is not what

God wants, but that doesn't mean He can't use the ugly parts to make something beautiful of them." And He is using her husband and her own body to live that out for their sweet girl. Imperfections and all.

How are you responding to the ugly parts in your life? How is God manifesting Himself in those hollow spaces? Do you notice and acknowledge how He reflects your created worth when you glance in the mirror? Where you see blemishes, He sees a tender perspective. Where you cringe at baldness, He sees bravery. Where you critique your body with scrutiny in the name of beauty, He stamps His image staring back at you and proclaims, *"I. am. pleased."*

One day Jamie and Doug will tell Norah about Jamie's struggles and how God used Doug to affirm Jamie's authentic beauty. And Donna doesn't miss an opportunity to walk alongside cancer patients, listening, loving them, looking in their eyes and telling them, "You are brave and beautiful."

The other night I tried to share the undie therapy story with Tanner and Ty, but I had barely gotten past the first word before they doubled over in eruptive laughter, their heads bowed above half-eaten plates. "Undies. Hahaha! You said 'undies.'" Gotta love boys. One day they'll get it. One day they'll understand about how their daddy was used in substantial ways to reflect real beauty to my broken soul and blemished body.

Does God care about the moments we feel ugly, unworthy, and less than? Absolutely! And He graciously reminds us not to focus on how others look, because we all know that's most likely not an accurate picture of what's going on inside. You know what God values most? Our hearts. "People look at the outward appearance, but the LORD looks at the heart"

(1 Samuel 16:7). *Well, that's a relief.*

God enters the scene, whatever bumpy and blemished circumstance we're in, and shows up in the form of others. Be it strangers, spouses, or friends, He speaks beauty and worth assurance through a hug, a cupped face, or eye contact. It's here Jesus reflects what so many of us need—physical touch, verbal words, real eyes to match His truth—spoken words we read about in scripture or sing about in church, but sometimes don't we just need a flesh-and-blood soul who can concretely connect the truth dots?

Before you crawl into bed tonight, whose face do you sense God putting in front of you? Who might be in an uncomfortable season of loss or illness or self-image traps and would benefit from God using you as a palpable megaphone to shout loud, "You are beautiful, and your life is made up of unconditional worth." What if you gift her an indulgence, like a party favor for surviving an ugly day, celebrating her significance when she most needs it? Maybe you bring her a slice of "just because" cake, or call her with affirmation and encouragement, or deliver flowers to her doorstep (with a note to save the petals after and scatter them as confetti to dress up Taco Tuesday dinner). Or maybe you slip some money in a gold envelope and mark it "For days when nothing but undie therapy will do."

6
COZY CORNER BOOTH

An Invitation to Community in the Midst of Loneliness

We have all known the long loneliness and we have learned that the only solution is love and that love comes with community.
—Dorothy Day

After dropping Ty off at school with his promise, "Mom, I will not smooch anyone today," giddiness took over. With the boys in all-day school (cue angels singing), nothing makes my heart happier than breakfast dates, this particular morning, with Cathy. Syrup and coffee fragrances welcomed as I swung open the door to our usual meeting spot. Tucked behind the host stand I noticed her perched in hidden seats. She was flapping her arms like a baby bird, beckoning me toward her. I scooted into the tiny booth, and she leaned forward, all smiles. "I prayed for this booth," she said with a smile. "I wanted something in the corner, tiny and cozy and intimate." The idea of engraving our names on a plaque and claiming it as ours crossed my mind. To make it official, of course.

"Of course you did." We laughed and ordered our typical plates. Hers, a veggie omelet with black olives instead of mushrooms. And for me, scrambled eggs and pancakes. "And coffee," we said in unison. "Please, for the love, Carlos, coffee." Our favorite waiter grinned and returned with those white café mugs that fit perfectly in our palms.

We shared in fast-forward, shoveling limited time in hungry gulps. We talked of work and what she and her hubby, Eric, were learning. About how our boys were somehow allergic to listening. We talked about marriage and couch dates and fighting for intentionality in a chaotic season with school and sports and full schedules.

Cathy recently passed her therapist's test and was now officially a marriage and family therapist, which makes sense, because the girl has the gift of seeing into one's soul in the best way possible. Like she's protecting a fragile egg. She is an incredible question asker and equally hilarious. We have way too much fun over breakfast and constantly have to stop ourselves from jumping up and down and scaring small children who are trying to enjoy their chocolate chip pancakes. *Yes, little ones, enjoy those pancakes. And ask for whipped cream while you're at it.*

On this particular day, we were so deep in conversation that our eggs grew cold and our mugs had been refilled at least ten times (cheers, Carlos) when I began crying. Ya know, *those* tears I didn't know lay dormant until I gave them words. "I'm lonely," I admitted. "I'm praying about who my people are, and I'm having a hard time figuring it out." I'd recently gone back to work, and in between speaking and writing, no longer doing playdates, and trying to give time to my hubby and boys, well, there didn't seem to be a lot of extra. Yet, I *adore* people. I *need* my peeps. And in addition to Bryan, I especially need girlfriends. The kind that I can be honest and real with without feeling like I have to be put together or stylish or witty. The kind of intimacy Donald Miller speaks of in *Scary Close*: "It's a beautiful moment when somebody wakes up to this reality, when they realize God created them so other people could enjoy them, not just endure them."[15]

"What does it feel like?" Cathy asked. You see what she did there? She's so dang good.

Lonely feelings tumbled out. "I feel like I've set this large banquet table with my favorite china and champagne flutes and striped linen napkins. And there are peony centerpieces and butter dishes. Butter dishes, people, because no meal is complete unless there is good bread on your plate to be buttered. And I'm sitting at this grand table, and no one is occupying the seats. I threw a dinner party and no one is coming."

At this point, I realize ugly crying has taken over, and I'm madly wiping snot on my sleeve, ever so aware that every person who walks into the restaurant sees my face directly behind the host stand. *Welcome to the Original Pancake House. We serve snot in your syrup.*

Here's one of the millions of ways I know Cathy is a dear friend. I can be completely messy and in process, and she loves me unconditionally. She offers safety and permission, and I don't feel like I have to produce eloquent words or well-thought-out sentences to entertain her. She offers a safe nest to share and think—one that's protected from harsh realities and winds of judgment. We all need safe people we can snotty cry with, amen?

"Oh, friend." She teared up, not out of pity but compassion. I could tell she was thinking, searching for the right words as she listened. "I wonder"—I love how she thinks aloud while silently praying and offers thoughts across the table. "I'm curious if perhaps Jesus wants to first sit with you at a cozy corner booth like this one, and over time will provide the right people in the right seats. Maybe your dinner party isn't a long banquet table for many but an intimate corner booth for the two of you first."

God is so very gentle when He shows up and His Spirit speaks through people. And her words were His, abundant with truth and relief. All my life, I thought loneliness was solved with *more* faces, *more* bodies, *more* relationships and stories. Like an overflowing Norman Rockwell painting with people crammed in seats, sharing hearty food and robust drinks. But as Cathy shared, I knew she was right. Until I find community enough in being with Jesus first, the entire restaurant wouldn't suffice the aching that loneliness hungers to fill.

In Luke 14, the parable of the great banquet paints a similar vision to how I was dreaming my life would appear: large, full, fancy. And then reality hits. Every single person the party planner invited came up with an excuse. You know this feeling, right? And what did the master do? He instructed his servant:

> "'Go out quickly into the streets and alleys of the town and bring in the poor, the crippled, the blind and lame.'
> "'Sir,' the servant said, 'what you ordered has been done, but there is still room.'
> "Then the master told his servant, 'Go out to the roads and country lanes and compel them to come in, so that my house will be full. I tell you, not one of those who were invited will get a taste of my banquet.'" (verses 21–24)

Okay, wow. So here's this guy—let's imagine our spouse or dad as the owner of the home, the inviter of the great banquet—and every empty chair signifies a no-show. *So rude.* And what does he do? He invites the lowest of the low to occupy the chairs, eat delectable delicacies, and sip the finest wines (I'm thinking of the recent bottle of Conundrum I've added to my fave red blend list), to come and celebrate at his feast.

Imagine the table that night—people who were suffering and hurting and unseen being welcomed and entertained at the table of this master. It's like if Bry went out and invited all the homeless, disabled misfits of Orange County and they came to the Pogue Cottage for tri-tip, salad, and fireside s'mores. Do you think they'd enjoy it more than our usual peeps? I can only imagine the conversations, how their bellies, hearts, and minds would be satiated in physical and emotional ways.

This is how the Spirit makes Himself real in our loneliness. He invites, and similar to those guests, how we respond affects how much we get to enjoy the taste of God's great banquet. *Gosh, I don't want to miss out.*

Dry is the season of loneliness. But ironically, it's the dry parts that lead to the sweetest understandings. We can't reach the good stuff unless we are willing to be aware that the hard stuff is, in fact, hard. *Isolating.* Maybe solitary isn't something we need to run away from, but an indication to run toward Someone. So it is with noticing my loneliness and recognizing how God is wooing me toward Him. Instead of wallowing or surrounding myself with more people, believing the illusion that more is better—*more* friends, *more* ministry, *more* success, *more* words, *more* media—I find truth in Cathy's words. And the truth is: I am not alone. Ever. *Never ever.*

When isolated, I-feel-alone thoughts hover, I began asking myself, *Am I lonely or just scared to be alone?* I realize I don't need *more* people—I need a few, close, safe ones. You know what Jesus reminds me of when I most crave connection? Intimate, not scattered-shallow, "I know of you but don't really know you" acquaintances. No, I crave deep, "this is who I am and who you are, and we genuinely enjoy and value each other" type of friends. And since Jesus is the author of relationships and community, being that He's part of the Trinity and all, I trust He cares that I desire connection because He created me this way—for relationships, for one another.

The desire for connection invites me to ask the One I find enough, *Who are my safe, truth-telling people?* Finding comfort with Jesus first brings this clarity. Where I find solace in a cozy corner booth. Where sweet connection and protected conversation may at first appear trivial—unlike fancy, merry group settings—it's here I find one-on-one connection to be the most intimate.

How I pray to saturate my mind with the words written in Joshua 1:9: "Have I not commanded you? Be strong and courageous. Do not be afraid; do not be discouraged, for the LORD your God will be with you wherever you go." Jesus is *with* us. He is *for* us. He longs to pull up a cozy chair for a one-on-one. From there, I trust my people are an overflow of His goodness, not a trophy to be earned.

That morning I left breakfast inspired to shift my perspective when lonely. And later it was actually a therapist who averted my misconception and pointed me toward a life-changing read that radically altered the title of "loneliness" and sanded it to shine "solitude." I'm sure it had nothing to do with snotty crying on her couch about this isolated tendency of mine. "I recommend Henri Nouwen's *Reaching Out*," she said with a gentle smile.

Henri (we would be on a first name basis if he were still alive) said, "The roots of loneliness are very deep and cannot be touched by optimistic advertisement, substitute love images or social togetherness."[16] He goes on to write about the brave faith required to lean into loneliness when everything in us wants to flee or ignore. He encourages us to "protect it and turn it into a fruitful solitude," one where hidden beauty is discovered in the desert. From here "the movement from loneliness to solitude, is the beginning of any spiritual life because it is the movement from the restless senses to the restful spirit, from the outward-reaching cravings to the inward-reaching search, from the fearful clinging to the fearless play."[17]

Oh, Henri, thank you.

Good-bye, loneliness. Hugs, solitude.

Instead of mourning empty chairs, I now long to scoot into a corner booth and be thankful for the Divine, who always sits there. And He inches close and says, *"You are never alone. Even if you feel it. I am still here.* And then He reveals who He places in my path. Our neighbors, the unassuming soul at work, a longtime college friend. *"Do you see who I continually pop in your coming and going? As you go about your life, there they are, showing up just around the bend. Do you see them? They are your hand-picked community."*

Why do I dream about so many friends "out there," when in reality, I needn't look farther than the two feet around me? How I desire to embrace the people I encounter and be present with those I'm actually with—not the ones I've ideally prepared a table setting for. When I stop fighting for more community and instead appreciate the few that God reserves at my booth, aloneness transforms to appreciation for those here in this moment—a small, safe-knit community that resembles a perfectly built nest.

And friends often come in surprising ways, as my friend Karen has taught me. As newlyweds, she and Shane were stationed in France for three years with the US Army. "With military life, you have to jump in. Having somebody is better than having no one, and I found community in people I wouldn't normally gravitate toward. You never know how you'll grow until you open yourself up. Community is everything," she shared. A foreign, French setting (just like in the movies) seemed dreamy as I sat in my living room surrounded by children's books and tiny boys. But Karen was always honest about the temptation to withdraw and let loneliness and an unknown tongue and no soul friends keep her from experiencing life to the fullest.

Karen met military wives in the small town of Lille, and although I imagined her becoming besties with the neighborhood baker, she brought reality to the forefront in admitting that some of the people she unexpectedly met there she wouldn't have necessarily been friends with in the States. "You don't have to be best friends, but you can learn a lot from people." And so Karen spoke with them. She and Shane invited them into their small French flat for dinners and playdates and an American Thanksgiving. They created a safe place for people to talk and share and be. They inspired a cozy corner booth right in their own home.

Regardless of half-finished projects, messes, and chaos, I'm inspired to open our home in the same way. To those I wouldn't expect to be friends with, I swing open the door and welcome them to our table, to our couch, and into our lives.

Karen inspired me to invite others into our cottage without expectation of reciprocation. "Sometimes people don't know how to host. So we invite and they come, and community is born." Karen looks back at those years in France with fondness, and it's the people she remembers. France is where she and Shane learned their gift of hospitality and practiced it with everyone from military spouses to captains to new parents. "Creating a place where people feel at home and welcome— that is the start of faith," Karen said.

I wonder if God plops people in our lives at dry seasons to remind us of His personal care and desire to be near. If we weren't ever alone, we wouldn't ever need Him, or then experience a deeper faith through His people.

Megan, my godsister, is like the sister I never had. She lives out her singleness, often associated with loneliness, in selfless, noticeable ways. A self-admitted romantic, she has always dreamed about her Prince Charming and a fairy-tale marriage. "Things weren't working out as I planned them to be. At thirty, it's not what I thought. I'm racing against time, family, relationships, feeling behind at every bridal and baby shower. But the idea of falling in love with God first has changed my thinking. With a man, I have the tendency to give it my all. It's been a process to figure out if my relationship with God really does come first. I know in the long run, this will be my biggest takeaway. My dependence on Him—I know I'll be better because of it. There's a lot that can make me feel lonely, or different, or like something is wrong with me. Really, it comes down to God's faithfulness, how He gives me space to recognize relationships instead of sulking," she shared.

At first Megan justified the fact that she isn't married with the reality that she can travel more. But then God planted the idea in her head: *"You are going to do great things, and you have to trust Me in the process."* Oh, the process. She transforms her loneliness into investing in others. She now sees her singleness as a gift, one that's given her time to devote to her family and be the involved auntie she wants to be. The idea of being available to help someone in a desperate time of need drew her in, and Megan volunteers as a certified crisis counselor at the Orange County Rape Crisis Center, often working the midnight shift. She paused, and I could hear the emotion in her voice when she resumed talking. "In terms of loneliness, when I have the opportunity to meet with someone who is isolated, and just sit with them, it gives me purpose. It's not about how many people; the important moments are those spent one-on-one with someone. The minutes I identify with someone else's story are the most impactful."

Megan now looks at her life through the perspective of, *Who would care if I were no longer around? Would I be missed?* "That idea is more driving than starting my own family. I want my mark to be bigger on the world. I'm so thankful I have the time to do it. Getting involved in church or community crisis centers or going on trips and getting to see where God is involved with this whole world proves my life is turning out better than my limited vision of hoping to get married and start a family. In a roundabout way, I'm thankful."

Perhaps community is one or two chairs pulled close with people we wouldn't necessarily choose, maybe even those on the outskirts who He hand picks for us, and us for them. Perhaps community isn't a large banquet table but a cozy corner booth, one where we come to know His intimacy and truth.

What if we join Jesus at the small table first? What if learning to be comfortable with the One will teach us to be grateful when there's more than one? How I hope to be ever so aware that Jesus occupies the seat next to me and is pulling out chairs as He sees fit. May I have eyes to see and a heart to accept, give back, and love, knowing community begins with the One. And then one person at a time.

Preferably ones who enjoy chocolate chip pancakes. With whipped cream.

7
#REALISTHENEWPERFECT

An Invitation to Find Freedom in an Online Culture

A real spiritual life. . .makes us so alert and aware of the world around us, that all that is and happens becomes part of our contemplation and meditation and invites us to a free and fearless response.

—Henri Nouwen, *Reaching Out*

*D*uring a family outing to the pumpkin patch, I became keenly aware of my social media struggle: *Portray perfection versus share what's real.* We pulled into a dusty, gravel-crunching parking lot and saw darling families donned in boots, plaid shirts, and floppy hats. They looked like they'd stepped out of a J.Crew ad. They even emitted hot apple cider aromas and all things pumpkin pie-ish. We? We were a ragamuffin crew. Not color coordinated, we appeared to be dunked in various buckets of navy; no mustard hues or sepia sweaters here. My hair? Birds currently took residence in its four-day-old fro. After all, we were going to the pumpkin patch for a family outing, not a photo shoot. But, friend, doesn't it usually lead to that?

The moment we *have* to capture! The perfect family photo! Said in a panicky voice to Bry: *"It's a holiday, and we need a Halloween picture in that cute frame your mom gave us."*

We spotted the ideal photo spot, near a scarecrow, of course. Every respectable family takes pictures next to an oversized, straw-stuffed, Raggedy Andy doll. A nearby sweet family with a newborn was our camera victim. "Would you mind taking our picture?" *My apologies, kind new father. This is your future.*

And so it began. "Mom *(whiny whine whine)*, the sun is in my eyes." "I'm hungry," came a higher-pitched voice. "Just smile," came my clenched reply. When the kind dad returned our camera and we clicked through each picture, *oh, you guys. So not pretty.* Bry appeared to be pinching Ty's neck for fear our little man would beeline it to the snack shop. Tanner's pale face looked like we forced him to watch a horror film. The whole thing? Comical and entirely *us*. Entirely *real*.

I had the gall, after thanking New Father for taking our picture, to bite my lip and squeak, "Would you mind taking one more? And this time"—I nudged Bry—"babe, could you not hunch over? Just stand up straight! Tanner, smile. Ty, stop covering your face."

In my head, I was allowing the idea of the perfect (what does that even mean?) family photo to hinder *our* family as it is. Lame, I know. Picture after imperfect picture reinforced how impossible it is to capture an ideal shot.

But I'm no quitter. *No, Mama's going to get a picture with her babies.* Because, let's be honest, I'm usually *behind* the camera. But nope, not today! "Come on, boys, let's take one together with your fave mum. You know, the one who carried and birthed you. And, T, remember you asked today where babies come from and we talked? Get up here"—I beckoned and pointed—"you owe me."

Every mom knows what follows: the squinty-eyed-mannequin-face, tickling-kids-to-grin-while-attempting-to-look-relaxed pose. *I'll buy you a pony if you please.just.smile.* Ty

104

booked it. Tanner physically removed my arm draped around his neck. And there I stood. Alone. Frustrated. Clearly *not* a hip, J.Crew parent.

Our pumpkin patch, real-life family picture evening was the straw that broke my perfect back. I mean, who was I kidding? Controlling attempts to capture an impeccable picture at the expense of *what*?

And so birthed the vision for #realisthenewperfect.

Real *is* the new perfect. The kind of authentic-reflecting real, where a freeing relationship dwells; where love, joy, peace, patience, and grace abide; where second, third, and fourth chances reside. As I live in awareness of how truly undeniably God relates, how He laughs and I recognize His comic heart while I'm crazily shouting at my kids in attempts to snag a smile, I aspire to reflect genuine laughter like His. I want to belly laugh about the whole hysterical ordeal. As I journey to see His heart smack dab in the middle of family pictures and social media, I'm inspired to settle into His perfection instead of attempting authenticity on my own.

Authentic. It's a ginormous buzzword in our technological age. Aren't we starving for genuine, unpolished, what's-really-going-on-behind-the-scenes connection? Have we mistaken authenticity as a permission slip to vomit our feelings in attempts of "being real"? Only when our true stories reflect a genuine Creator will social media invite and engage freedom. As my designer friend Annette wisely noted, "Let's use technology to inspire, not intimidate." To promote grace-filled online imperfections, to share the beauty of authenticity. To free us to inspire. Authenticity shares without fear of how it will be responded to.

With all the social networking websites on our lovely

World Wide Web, it's a miracle our computers and phones can hold all of the data without blowing to smithereens. Twitter, Facebook, Pinterest, LinkedIn, Instagram. (Do you guys know there's a website called Hedgehogs? Darling, isn't it?) In today's technological flurry, we can stay connected, research data from our porch swings, pin from Hawaii, and reconnect with old friends. We can Skype with overseas spouses and spread the Gospel faster than ever before. Social networking grows incredible social justice organizations and advances God's kingdom for the benefit of communicating across the globe.

We are *so* connected.

But are we *really*? We love us some social media; however, we are literally running to catch up with it in real time, responding and navigating to it as fast as the next app is downloaded. *Periscope. Check. Blog read. Check. Scroll Instagram. Scan Facebook. Comment. Like. What's happening on Pinterest? Check. Check. Check.* No wonder we don't have this dialed in. We're madly trying to stay current with every new thing that bursts into online existence.

Friends, the use of social media isn't the discussion. It's not like when I was in junior high and raised my hand to ask our youth pastor, "How far is too far?" The real questions are: "How authentic can I be online?" "How can I reflect my genuine story?" "How can I use my journey to inspire others with truth and freedom, not guilt and judgment?" "How present can I be to my life?" I'm so quick not to overspiritualize online culture, but the more time I spend on it, talk with women, notice a decline in deep relationships and an increase in depression, I'm convinced this amazing technological movement is a spiritual battle. Since any great idea is God's idea, why wouldn't the enemy use social media to distract and depress us where its intended purpose is for communication and deeper connection? What if we shifted our perspective and viewed this selfie culture not as good or bad, but as it's intended purpose: a tool? A tool we celebrate with truth, knowing the truth will set us free (John 8:32).

Freedom leads with open arms and absence of necessity, so it's a wonder our culture is a slave to social media when *how* we use this tool is *our* choice. Why are so many of us bogged down, overwhelmed, feeling "less than" after time spent online? Are we free or constrained by these decisions?

I sent a poll out to my peeps and posed the question "What are the biggest social media lies you believe? Go!" In a flash, my phone was vibrating, beeping, and hollering with responses.

I'm not enough. Neither are my spouse or kids.
I could and should be doing more.
Everyone else is having more fun. They are happier, richer, thinner, more creative, and their kids are perfect.
Everyone is hanging out together.
What I'm doing isn't as important or exciting as you.
Social media is the Perfect Comparison Game on repeat.
I have to be the best version of myself at all times.
I have to have a fascinating life, including lots of social engagements and activities to matter.
Being a mom is supereasy and fun all.the.time.
Everyone is dieting or training for marathons. And because of this, when they see me, they think I'm fat.

If I mattered, I'd have more followers, likes, comments, and shares.

Everyone is more put together, more organized, more important.

Well, don't you feel cozy? But seriously, we entertain these thoughts, don't we? At any given season, we may relate to each response. Those in child-rearing seasons see social media through the lens of a parent. Those who desire fitness filter news through nutrition, weight, and physical appearance. And those who are socially inclined are most aware of "what everyone is doing all the time." *Everyone. Always. All.* These words shine an accurate light on exaggerated feelings, which can be an innocent symptom of using social media. Suddenly reality is twisted through a perfect perception, leaving women overwhelmed and underinspired.

What's really *real?*

Real *is* the new perfect.

Perfection is found as I follow Jesus into the center of real life—social media included—and come to know His heart, one overflowing with freedom and peace. You want authenticity? Are you craving the genuine of all genuineness? Look no further than within, His dwelling place. Where God, the author of authenticity, the One who actually exists and is not imaginary or fake or artificial, resides. Imagine. Imagine what it looks like to grasp this truth. He first met me at a point where I had no spiritual, precious goods to make Him happy, and He wanted me all the more. It was *then* I experienced a relationship in normal, everyday ways. The further I clear away the distractions and closer I choose to find Him in details of today, I want nothing more than to echo His genuine Spirit. I want to be true and accurate and genuine, but only as a result of first drawing from His realness and living from an overflow with the one true God.

So how do we embrace #realisthenewperfect and find freedom in a selfie culture? I've found that three *T* words affect my mind and heart and relationships when it comes to social media: *triggers*, *truth*, and *time*.

Triggers

Like many fresh moms, I started blogging when we welcomed Tanner into our family. A way to document every urp and coo, I mostly wrote to process the gazillions of questions and thoughts and lessons I was learning. And of course, I pushed PUBLISH and found myself suddenly deep in the online vortex of Facebook, and articles, and blogs, and *Who is this person?* and *Why am I suddenly stalking her photos?* Don't laugh—you know you've done this.

The deeper I delved, the uglier the feelings that surfaced.

Loneliness.

Comparison.

Discontentment.

Do you relate?

I scrolled Instagram, paused, and listened to inner racket. *So-and-so is at the beach on a playdate. Why wasn't I invited?*

What's triggered? Loneliness.

Certain blogs pricked an unscratchable itch. *Wow, this blogger is crazy creative, and her tutorials are intricately detailed. How in the world does she find time to make fifty hand-stitched pillows per day, feed her children nutritionally organic meals, manage to have a perfect figure/marriage/home and a photography studio on the side?*

What's that, you lovely blog? Comparison.

Facebook-skimming sessions evoked my nastiest reactions. *Oh, look. She just bought a new house and put in hardwood floors and remodeled their kitchen; and did you see how it's decorated in all copper? Kill her!*

What's triggered? Discontentment.

Not to mention, it seems online connection has replaced real connection.

I began paying attention to thoughts, pricks, and reactions. I gathered each one and laid them on the table to take a deeper look. What stared back was the truth, that in a world where God desires to bring hope, comparison cobwebs easily tangle my perspective. Daily, I found my heart and mind surrounded by hundreds of social media triggers. Worse yet, I made conclusions based on what I read or saw. Do you find yourself doing this? Finding a need "to make up a story" as Brené Brown says in *Rising Strong*, based on fragments of photos, shared snippets, or circumstantial feelings?[18]

Yet I couldn't stop reading, scrolling, *scouring* the Internet. Social media became an addiction, my finger automatically pushing the Home button, tapping an app, or clicking computer keys. Where is freedom when I'm enslaved to a device?

I'd roll over first thing in the morning and reach for my phone resting on our nightstand. *Let's see. . .what's happening in the world.* Never mind that I was ignoring two adorable boys and my husband down the hall of *my* world.

How many likes do I have from last night? Comments? E-mails? Before my feet hit the carpet to walk into our sun-drenched kitchen to hug my family and see their eyes, my own eyes searched for worth *on.a.phone.*

At stoplights I checked texts.

During couch dates, I snuggled into Bryan, both of us married to our phones.

At the pumpkin patch, I shooed our kids away while I edited and posted a picture of our "amazing family moment" we clearly *were.not.having*.

I lived vicariously through social media, unaware I aimed my value in the response of people instead of the truth of who I know I am. *Freedom-offering? No siree.*

Jeff Shinabarger admits in *Yes or No*, "I struggle with this all the time. This morning, I looked to see how many people were following me on Twitter. I often check to see if anyone liked my latest photo. Too often I try to quantify my influence, and then it becomes a ranking game of me versus the rest of the world. . . . Why do I do these things that have no meaning?" And then I love how he drops this truth bomb: "Because I want to be known. I want to feel special, to feel loved and to feel self-worth. I want people to think I matter. There is something within us that wants attention."[19]

Guil. Tee. Why else do we share our stories and pictures and thoughts with the world, if not in hopes of connecting and receiving validation and affirmation? It's our human nature to connect, the creativity within us desiring cheers and applause. But when we base our value on another's response or lack thereof, we turn into crazy people pleasers. We become actors playing inauthentic roles instead of bringing our true selves to the stage, declaring, *Here I am. And it's so freeing to be genuinely me.*

Noticing these triggers, I chose to dig deeper to discover *why* they affected my mind and heart in extensive ways and saw that I was forgetting the authentic journey and focusing on projecting perfectionism.

Do you know when my perfection party is in full-on *go* mode? Valentine's Day. I'm no Valentine's Day hater. I adore all the sappy, lovey attributes sprinkled, wrapped, and displayed in vases for those we love. I just don't want it blowing up my news feed. But sure enough, in a weak moment, I hopped online, and *bam!* Staring back at me were sentiments and adoration from a husband toward his wife, and I perch like a falcon on our leather chair ready to attack my husband the minute he walks in the door from work. Which occurred approximately two minutes later.

My beak was in his face as soon as he entered. Nearly gave the poor man a heart attack. *Ah! Hey.* He leans back 'cuz I look like I'm going to devour him, and not in a romantic way. I hold my phone like prey, my eyes glowing, feathers standing straight up. I'm practically molting, people.

"Why," I say through a clamped jaw. "Why didn't you put a picture up of me for Valentine's Day and say what a wonderful wife and cook and mom and. . . ?" My voice trails off because I'm watching the crazy scene unfold in slow motion and *I'm in it.* (Side note: that's when you know it's pathetic.)

He took in a deep breath and cautiously joined me on the leather chair. "Wow," he exhaled. "I didn't post something online because I tell you how much I love you every day. I don't need the rest of the world to know what goes on between us. I like protecting our marriage and keeping some things private."

So I pecked his eyes out.

There's truth in his words, though. We've become a culture that likes to share real-time emotions and feelings when there may be value in experiencing, holding close, and keeping words private. An *aha* moment experienced alone or with another doesn't need a stamp of approval from anyone on social media. Sharing to inspire can be beautiful, and wisdom led from silence, a double gift.

I talked with friends about our shared online tussles. "I'm striving for perfection but wanting real at the same time." Aloud, I processed through negative emotions when they surfaced, and I asked myself, *Why am I anxious when I see certain photos? Why do some posts trigger inadequacies and lies that I'm "less than"? What's at the root of these emotions? And why do I care?*

As I chose to walk into the center of these mind and heart triggers, I recognized my insecurities: perfectionism, the temptation to be everywhere with everyone, and confusing my identity with how Jesus sees me versus how others respond. What emotions are triggered when you spend time on social media? How does being online affect your head and heart?

Guess what? We have a choice with how to respond to social media triggers. When your inner falcon emerges, it's most likely a warning sign to pay attention. Does being online bring out a genuine version of yourself, or would "unplugging" be in your best interest? Some days we are indestructible, while other days our humanness gets provoked and *we.just.can't. handle* the feelings stirred inside. Gustav Mahler, an Austrian composer and conductor said, "The point is not to take the world's opinion as a guiding star, but to go one's way in life and work unerringly, neither depressed by failure nor seduced by applause."[20] Social media isn't good guys versus the bad guys. It's a platform for human opinions and creativity. The more I care about what Jesus thinks, the less social media has power over my thoughts and emotions.

Truth

How do we embrace #realisthenewperfect when it comes to relationships—primarily our relationship with Jesus? A question I ask daily is, *Where am I going for truth?* Truth brings freedom and cements my identity. And truth can come only from the Creator. Am I making time for Him or spending my "free" time online? When I looked back at my involvement online, I noticed feeble attempts for worth strokes and truth teachers. The honest reality? Only Jesus is the Truth—the Author, the Healer, and the Promise of Enough. No comment, article, quote, picture, oohs, aahs, shares, or likes will offer certainty that you are worthy and enough.

The more I asked myself the truth question, the more I became aware of where I was seeking validation. One afternoon I was walking down our short hallway to put the boys' laundry on their beds when I heard God speak aloud, *"Why aren't I enough?"* My steps stilled, closet mirrors reflecting hands that carried folded T-shirts and Big Hero 6 undies.

"Why aren't *You* enough?" I echoed back. Wow. All this time I was focusing on social media from my perspective, and here was God asking if there was room for Him to be enough. Truth bombs. He drops them even in laundry piles and hallway conversations. The truth is that no one, no social media avenue, will ever be enough. And even though God created community and connectedness and inspires technology to be reflective of His good, until my identity is found completely in Him, I'll still search for truth in other venues.

When I pay attention to how triggers evoke lies and turn them over to my Father, He offers peace. When I search for unconditional enoughness and truth online, I don't like the version of Bekah I become. But, when I go to Jesus' words for truth first, being aware of Him with all my senses, I notice the value in Proverbs 27:19: "As water reflects the face, so one's life reflects the heart." *Boom*. Truth experienced from the Father shares truth. Truth sought online leaves users with temporary satisfaction resulting in cravings hours later.

How does your relationship with technology reflect you? Your heart? Your truths? In the book *7* by Jen Hatmaker, she calls out addictive symptoms noted by scientists who confirm that multitasking with various mediums of information is harming our ability to focus. When information comes to us, we feel an urgency to respond immediately, similar to what runners experience with a runner's high—a dopamine squirt of adrenaline. Not only can these impulsive reactions become addictive, but when the stimulation isn't met, a bored sensation overrules, leaving a high percentage of our society stunted emotionally, relationally, and creatively.[21]

We have become a society that is bored and therefore dependent on entertainment, escape, and numbing through technology. Ironically, truth is nowhere near boring and, when sought, fills instead of empties, inspires instead of discourages, and embraces instead of numbs the life we already have.

Speaking of bored, an East Coast professor, Sherry Turkle, wrote an article for *Real Simple* on the fallout of technology. She talked about how "there's less tolerance for the boring parts of life." Part of her fieldwork was to stand at stoplights and observe what people do in their cars. You know where this is going. What do we do when we roll to the red hexagon? We grab our phones. Sherry noticed people can't be alone with their thoughts. Heaven forbid we are bored for .2 seconds. She encourages parents "to show kids that there's no need to panic if we're without our phones. If you don't teach children it's okay to be alone, they'll only know how to be lonely."[22]

We can't be alone. We can't be still. We.must.reach.for. the.closest.technological.device (*said in a robot voice*). Do you ever feel like a robot? Our kids don't know that our phones are simply tools, mere plastic devices. Wouldn't I laugh if my son walked around with a Lego spaceship—talking into it, staring at it, touching the round bumps, avoiding eye contact—because his Lego spaceship is obviously much more important than reading *Alexander and the Terrible, Horrible, No Good, Very Bad Day*? Yet I do that to him every day with a phone the size of twenty-five Lego pieces combined.

God, help me see how real You are when I take the time to be bored. To be still. Help me soak up Your truth in Psalm 46:10, urging, "Be still, and know that I am God." How am I to know You if I can't be still for .2 seconds to look up at the stop sign, smile at a child on the corner, notice birds perching in bushes, and hear You in quiet gulps? Where did I miss You in those blinks of time? What creative avenues of worship were You inviting me into when I went looking for authenticity on my phone?

I'm responding to our technological culture by choosing to put my phone in my purse when I drive, on the counter when I'm home, away when I'm with people. I'm choosing to honor what's real in the present, where #realisthenewperfect. It's not easy. I fight it. *Daily.* Especially when the boys get home from school and ask me to shoot hoops outside or to play Candyland. But the more I respond with a *yes*, a heart posture of being still, I learn to focus on them, their words, their hearts. It's difficult, because I'd rather grab my phone and escape on Instagram to see what people are designing in *their* dream homes or what my East Coast peeps are making for *their* dinner, or to smile at games other moms are playing with *their* darling children than to sit and play with my *own* kids in my *own* dust-bunnied cottage where my *own* Crock-Pot is cooking. These simple decisions are slowly molding me to be undisturbed, which translates into a spiritual stillness, a heart discipline. Being present helps me make room to hear God speak above the racket of social media fuzz. And each time I choose to be quiet, I find Him whispering freeing words: *"You know what's real? Playing Legos and shooting baskets and throwing frozen pizza in the oven for dinner. That, My daughter, is perfection."*

Time

I'm convinced time online affects our families. Valuable are the years God uses parenting, fostering, and grandparenting to build kids' faith foundations. Let's soak them up and choose to offer our presence. Every click of our phones is an audible reminder that our focus is drawn away from their curious faces and inquisitive questions.

As a writer, I work at home, which wasn't easy when the boys were younger. I was juggling research for talks and blogging, and I even did a short stint of overseeing social media for a magazine. With no boundaries, I felt overwhelmed. One day Tanner asked me to sit and play "guys" with him, and as we role-played with plastic superheroes, Pokémon characters, and whatever the current Happy Meal prize was, I asked, "T, how come you don't ask me to play 'guys' with you more?" Without missing a beat, he pointed to the computer at home on our kitchen table and sighed, "'Cuz you're always on that thing."

Ugh. Oh. Ouch. Truth—it will set us free.

From that moment on, I took a good hard look, evaluated

my priorities, and decided that although the days are long, the years are indeed short. Having a relationship with my sons, making myself available as a playmate, is more precious than pecking at computer keys. Ty often grabs my hand and asks, "Mom, come jump on the trampoline with me." You guys, playing and jumping are not my spiritual gifts—they don't come with enthusiasm or with passionate joy. But I do them because coming alongside what brings my sons joy speaks love. Now I write and prepare when they are at school, and once they are home, we do homework, shoot baskets, play at the park, and prep for dinner. Not spreading myself all over like confetti but homing in on who is in front of me and fostering that bond is focusing and freeing.

In the same breath, I'm an advocate for modeling how to live out my created self to our sons. Writing and speaking make me feel alive. They enable me to shine a facet that doesn't illuminate elsewhere. *Not at the expense of others, though.* When my boys do homework or paint rainbows at our table, I work alongside them. As I encourage them to live from their unique passions, God shines through each of us. If my life-giving work only reflects myself, if they don't feel the warmth of rays coming their direction, they'll have little appreciation for my talents, and my time will be misspent.

Do you let your kids into your work? If you're a writer, read them your work. If you're a teacher, share a mini lesson plan. If you're a rockstar stay-at-home mom with kids in school, tell them stories about your day. What may seem boring to you interests curious ears. Invite them onto your lap and share what spills out of your heart. Invite them into your classroom. Invite them into the kitchen. In the same way we long to know about their day, they, too, want to know us, including our passions. Be mindful of your time and how you are communicating how you spend it. If our children only see us on our phones and computers, they start to believe these devices are more important than they are.

We see how time online affects our kids because it affects us as adults, and we have the maturity to choose how to spend our hours. That is why stepping in front of this real-time selfie culture to model boundaries to our children and ourselves is critical. Bry worked in youth ministry for fifteen years and saw the mounting pressure technology placed on kids and culture. When we hand children a phone, it's easy to forget that we are handing them access to the Internet and they aren't equipped with how to process and respond to what bombards them unless we prepare them. What if our focus isn't, *That online (fill in the blank situation) won't happen,* but instead, *When that happens, I'll prepare my son or daughter with how to navigate the feelings and choices that surface.* As we evaluate where time is spent, most likely we will find where our treasure is also.

After speaking about social media effects with a group of moms, we discussed how those effects applied to our kids in real life. One mom blurted out, "My daughter lost her phone and threatened to commit suicide."

Wait. What? When did technology root such despair that we no longer want to live based on its availability? The cure isn't to throw the phones in the trash or to forbid our kids to use social media, or to turn a blind eye, pray they don't look at porn, and live in ignorant bliss. The cure is talking with our kids about *what* they will see, *how* they will feel, and *why* it's important to make the most of their time online. We have seen, felt, and struggled with the same, and we are older, wiser, and have age spots to prove it. Let's teach them to use social media as a freeing benefit, not a detriment to their lives.

Let's model how to communicate verbally—how to look one another, adults, and authority figures in the eyes. Let's lead by asking questions, showing how to be comfortable without a device to distract from real-time conversation. The younger we start these practices, the more confident our children will be seeing a person, not a screen, in front of them.

Later in Sherry Turkle's *Real Simple* article, she responds to the question "Why has texting become more common than talking?" "Because it protects people from the possibility of confrontation. There's a whole generation that isn't learning how to have a conversation." She asked kids why they avoid, face-to-face communication, and they said, "It takes place in real time and you can't control what you're going to say."[23] If we don't help kids develop these skills, they won't be prepared to navigate online culture.

How do we prepare them? We share our stories, our struggles, our imperfections. Bryan had the opportunity to be a part of postcollege interviews, asking young adults questions about specific parts of their faith journey. You know what every person shared? They wished their parents had been more vocal and vulnerable about their imperfections. They longed to witness their parents struggle with faith the same way they were and to understand struggling is a necessary, normal process. But what they saw at home, and even online, didn't match up. Projecting perfectionism was the main entrée they were served, and they were starving for authenticity. Bry came home that day on a mission, and we may have swung the pendulum the other way, letting our boys see our in-the-process mess, our flaws highlighted.

Truth be told, I'd rather them go to therapy for talking too much about feelings than pushing them aside. I'd rather remind them to seek perfection from Jesus, not a shiny, perfection-portraying online culture, regardless of how *real* they are led to believe it is.

Mother Teresa said, "Love begins at home, and it is not how much we do. . .but how much love we put into that action."[24] You know how we model love to our kids? *Time.* We love them with our minutes, hours, and days. We offer real. We teach them how to use technology as a tool. We step in front of their questions and answer with our faulty experiences and validate what they will wrestle with. We give them permission to crave credibility and remind them that truth comes not from a tiny device but from an omnipotent God.

Spearheading #realisthenewperfect, inviting others to share, and learning from women's stories, here are practical changes our family is making when it comes to technology:

- Modeling how to follow the driving rules. I try to avoid texting when driving or checking my phone at stop signs. Our kids watch everything. Like that one time I got pulled over for texting on the way to speak about social media? Ain't no perfection here.

- Teaching our kids to use their creativity when bored, alone, or experiencing downtime. We don't need to be entertained. We grab a book, a ball, a brush and imagine.

- Sharing and inviting our kids to value the beauty of real connections.

- Keeping our phones on vibrate.

- Removing Facebook from my phone and turning off Instagram notifications.

- Assuming the motto "Post, then be present."

- Putting computers away and phones in a vintage soup bowl from dinner until bedtime. Those are sacred family hours. If there's a need, it can wait until the kids are sleeping.

- Teaching our boys the phrase "Be with the people you're with" and leading from that belief.

- Inviting our kids into our work. I read them my blogs and talks, and Bryan shares work projects. We let them ask questions and be a part of our passions.

- Creating adventure before rewarding online time.

- Celebrating how technology is a fun treat, not an entitlement or right; a tool, not a trophy.

- Championing how to change the selfie culture from *me* to *He*.

Social media is a great tool for staying connected, and freedom comes when we refuse to buy the lies that it replaces people or defines reality. As I lean into awareness of how triggers, truth, and time affect my mind and heart and my relationships, online opportunities inspire, not overwhelm. At the end of my life, God doesn't care about my followers. He cares about the One I chose to follow.

See you at the pumpkin patch, friends. We'll be the family dressed in teal, offering to take your pictures. Long live #realisthenewperfect.

8
COMMUNICATING VALUE

*An Invitation to Deeper Relationships
in the Midst of Tension*

*The one whose walk is blameless, who does what is righteous, who
speaks the truth from their heart; whose tongue utters no slander,
who does no wrong to a neighbor, and casts no slur on others. . . .
Whoever does these things will never be shaken.*
—Psalm 15:2–3, 5

I'm looking for connection and intimacy," she bravely
shared. She's a new friend, her perspective both
refreshing and welcome. We stroll Balboa Island, our
boys running ahead then jumping off ledges, footprints
carving sandy paths toward the calm water. She admits she's
unsure about religion yet carries an openness for something
more, a hope for deep, vulnerable friendships. Her words
resonate to my core. *Isn't that what Christianity is—an
intimate relationship with Real?* A true, back-and-forth, give-
and-take relationship? The type where hearts are searched to
be understood, known, and valued?

Sounds dandy on paper, right?

Have you ever believed that if we're Jesus followers and
people lovers, we'll avoid relational conflict and conversational
tension and just go around loving each other constantly?
Bahaha! So comically precious, isn't it? Until I look around
and notice unique personalities and various upbringings,

opinions, and thoughts. News flash: we humans are bound to disagree, hurt one another, and carry unspoken expectations. May I offer us permission to celebrate *when*, not *if*, conflict occurs as an invitation to create deeper relationships by communicating value?

Good old-fashioned communication, *I tell ya*. The kind where we exchange information back and forth, and with it, the risk of miscommunication in the form of expectations, assumptions, and those lovely moments of tension we've all experienced. Like the time Bryan and I assumed the other was watching our then two-year-old son, Tanner, and *lost him for almost forty-five minutes in Newport Beach.*

"I thought you had him!" he panicked.

"I thought you had him!" I yelled.

It's always fun to be reunited with a child thanks to a neighborhood search and a kind police officer. Did I mention we lost him on Mother's Day? Yes, you may forge ahead to read the parenting chapter now. Oh wait. There *isn't* one.

Dang relationships. They require much communication. And whether you hope for intimacy with two or twenty, it takes a lot of hard work. I'm finding that communication is like cake, and I'm talking about Miss Chocolate Layered Cake sitting on her pedestal, taunting me until the final hour when the guests are allowed to dig in. The deeper I choose to progress through one relational layer after another—through expectations, through tension, assumptions, and awkward conversations—frosting the entire stack of love with clarifying questions, the more satisfying it becomes. At this point, I'm all in, covered in rich, relational heaven, you could say.

It's here that the idea of communicating value sparked. Because it's one thing to make a cake and set it down in front of a friend and say, "Enjoy." But what if she enjoys a one-layer cake while another person desires a ten-layer cake? Relationships vary from one person to the next, which is why valuing each one in her unique way requires effort. I can't expect to throw words at someone and catch a dynamic relationship in return. I'm talking about desiring intimate, "this hard work is worth it" relationships. *Real*ationships, if you will. When we choose to connect with one another through listening and sharing, we are changed *for* it, *from* it, and better understand God's heart *in* it. Communicating value is more than showing someone love; it's wanting that person to feel known, heard, valued in her unique way, no matter how imperfectly said.

When relationships require little effort, I cruise along at status quo. But when they get tricky, I'm in the process of learning how to see that person the way Jesus sees her. I can do this only if I know my Father in an intimate way first. When I bring my awkward words and expectations to Him, I find safety, grace, and acceptance. He doesn't order me around or dismiss my thoughts. He leads with devotion, one that's reciprocal. Because I can go deep in a relationship with my Father, I hope to experience an overflow of that same connection with my husband, family, and friends.

If God's first priority is relationships, why not take my hurts and fears and expectations to Him and start with, "Okay, God, this feels really awkward," and let Him speak His thoughts before I react? When I respond with Holy Spirit–saturated words, I'm finding they come from a place of heart connection, not control. I used to freak out when tension rose, and would attempt to repair relationships on my own. I'm learning as I experience a sincere relationship with God that He actually wants to join me as I communicate my heart to others. When I tune my communication filter through His, I'm more aware of listening, hearing, and letting God refine relational circumstance. When I panic because it's weird, I go into crazy, fix-it mode, centered on my control, not His. I'm over ugly conversations. Bring on communicating value.

Communicating value begins with asking simple questions: "How do you feel valued?" "How can I best understand your heart in this moment?" "How can I peer past this tension and respond in love, knowing God adores us the same and wants us to move toward this relational thing?"

*Real*ationships happen on purpose. They take fighting for, seeing past, peering through, and communicating with, especially when messy. Deep connection is created when I honor the purpose of true intimacy by valuing you as much as I value myself.

I used to believe, when panicky tension indicated a relational rift, *I'm a fraud. I don't know how to do relationships. If I'm following after Jesus, I won't have disruptions in friendships.* Ha, ha, belly laugh, ha. Where do I get the idea that faith equates peace with *all* people at *all* times?

Fraud is a strong word, but honestly, it's the first that came to mind. My former relational misconception hinged on the belief *If I'm genuine, I'll do relationships perfectly.* I don't know where I got this mind-set that I'm supposed to have it all dialed in, but here's the truth: relationships take work. Vulnerability—risk of putting myself out there, with no control for how another will respond—*terrifies* me. It's much easier to people-please my way through life, but there, true peace lacks. It's a facade I have to keep up, and looking back, I excelled at codependent connection in my younger years. I learned to shine a fun, go-with-the-flow role, which kept me at first-bite-of-cake level. *Boring.*

The last couple of years, my go-to question when a relational circumstance isn't going as planned is, *Where is God in this fragile friendship?* And I've especially found myself asking this when it comes to the work of communication. *God, how can I know Your heart better as I make my way into the messy layers of not-so-easy relationships?* These days I'm no longer interested in tossing safe sentences back and forth but in communicating *value.* And by its definition, value is "the importance or worth of something," and what could be a more worthwhile investment than people? Okay, maybe desserts, but I don't whisper sweet nothings to gooey brownie sundaes.

Are we to communicate value to every person? Go deep with all people? What about those who are not safe or kind or beneficial to be with? *Are you telling me to get all cozy with those peeps?* That, my friend, is *your* confident call. Only you can decide who your people, your soul sistahs are.

My friend Stacie refers to her people as those on her "short list." My peeps? They are "my nest." I used to view relationships in an unhealthy balance, as if it was my job to invest deeply with every person I came in contact with. I practically gave myself an early heart attack attempting to be besties with the postman and new neighbor. It was Cathy who helped me understand connection with a freeing perspective. She encouraged me to view friends in varying levels of intimacy. There are the people I invite on the front lawn and sip iced tea with, and when we do, it's great. There are those I invite inside to plop on the couch and enjoy coffee and brownies with. We go deeper, share more, and choose to know each other more sincerely. The intimacy circle shrinks as I invite others into my kitchen. These friends know where the lemon squeezer, hand mixer, and funky straws are. They make themselves at home in our tight spaces, and we laugh when we booty-bump each other opening drawers. My kitchen people discover old leftovers in the back of my fridge. These souls don't have to live local for us to know our way around each other's wholehearted lives. And then there are the most intimate of friends I invite into our room in a relational sense. Aside from my husband, only they are welcome to walk in and see the laundry piles on our bed and take in all.the.mess. If they continue to come back, these cherished friends are officially "nearest and dearest."

Does that help you better know who is in your nest? Maybe take time to ponder and pray and ask yourself, *Who do I really long to do close relationship with, not just who do I see on a daily basis? If there's an emergency, who do I call? Who do I think of or communicate with on a deeper level? Who gets me inside and out, even if it's been six months since we last spoke?*

Heather is one of my nearest and dearest, and since our hilarious college roomie days, we've journeyed every pit and peak together. I've also learned over the years how she most feels valued as an introvert, one who pours her heart and soul into her family. She doesn't need anyone besides her sister and a local friend and a few of us scattered across the continent. I used to doubt our friendship because we didn't talk often, but she told me once, and I'll never forget, "I know you are my people, and knowing is better than anything."

When you know those in your nest, *and you will know*, it's *those* relationships you are choosing to communicate value to most.

Communicating value starts with Miss Chocolate Layered Cake's foundation: Expectations.

Expectations

When Bryan and I told our parents we were moving from our local, newlywed apartment in Brea four hours North to Atascadero, it was here the awareness of expectations came into play. My mom literally told my husband, "I feel like my right arm has been cut off." No exaggeration. And we laugh about it now, but at the time, that's exactly how she felt. In talking it over with them (years later, after her arm healed), we recognized expectations in full force. *We* had expectations for their reactions. Hopes that they'd jump up and down and wish us the best on our new adventure. Not so much. *They* had expectations that we would stay close, the same way their friends' kids did when they married.

What are you hoping for? Needing? Expecting? I notice when I mentally rehearse *shoulds*, my expectations are in the red. *She should call me. He should be more intuitive. They should ask about the kids.* By recognizing my expectations, I'm learning to place them in a healthy or unhealthy category and move forward. When I prop people on a pedestal taller than Miss Chocolate Cake, when I obsess about them, replaying conversations and analyzing every word until I feel insane, I know I've entered unhealthy expectation territory.

To discern whether expectations are valid or inching too close to an unhealthy ledge, I seek wisdom in the Psalms. "May these words of my mouth and this meditation of my heart be pleasing in your sight, Lord, my Rock and my Redeemer" (19:14). *God, how I want my words to be a beautiful overflow of my heart condition to You and to those I count dear.*

I'm finding it is never too late to start transforming my unhealthy expectations into healthy ones, and it begins when I verbalize my hopes and ask if they can be met. "I want to see you more. Does that work in this season?" "I'd love to connect for a phone date every few months." "I'd love to be more aware of what you're going through so I can love and support you. How can we do that? What are your thoughts?"

What are your expectations for your spouse? Your kids? Your parents? Your friends? Are they unhealthy or healthy? Do they know your expectations, and have you asked them theirs? When we communicate our hopes and needs, we communicate value. When I stuff my expectations, resentment builds. When I pull them out and hand them to another, I relieve us both from playing the guessing game. In return, I free the other person up to share her expectations. It's a win-win.

When Bryan and I married, we made the vow, "We won't play games," meaning we wouldn't expect the other person to be a mind reader and then punish him or her for a lack of psychic powers. Life is too short to build resentment for words not said. So we say it. *We say it all, friends.* And sometimes it's funny and downright punchy, and sometimes I've said things I wish I could retrieve and burn. Communication is not perfect; it's a process. Now we claim the phrase, "Unsaid expectations are unmet expectations." If I'm unable to stand back and even think about what I need and verbalize that, how on earth is my spouse supposed to meet my hope? *Impossible.* Friends, let's agree not to play games, and when we start feeling frustrated or even angry, let's communicate what we want. Most likely the soul standing on the other side of your conversation will thank you.

Oftentimes expectations surface unexpectedly. One of the surprising gifts of loss was losing my people-pleaser, fluffy filter. It died overnight, and I was forced to figure out how to communicate what I really needed and hoped for, and then do the hard work of grieving those expectations when they weren't met. I remember talking with a friend about expecting there to be the same amount of visitors reaching out physically or verbally after my dad died as there were when he was in the hospital. *I'm sure there will be tons of people stopping by or calling still.*

Reality offered another grief layer, rooting anger and bitterness. *Where is everyone?* I asked. Nothing reflects disappointment at unmet expectations more than hurt in the form of anger. I quickly learned to state my needs without shaming myself with the title *needy*. Having needs isn't needy; it's honest. And if my heart yearns to follow after Jesus, I am learning to be confident and vocal in my needs and then let Him meet me when those expectations aren't met. During this time, I called a wise therapist friend and shared my hurt at how few people were around in the fresh days and weeks of grief. "Where are they?" I cried scorching tears. "Why aren't they?"—my voice trailed as she offered experienced perspective. "Bekah, you are not the Holy Spirit. Much of your grief work will be not playing His role in others' lives. Let Him do what He's doing in you and trust He's got them, too."

Do you know the freedom her words offered? *You mean it's not my responsibility to care for all aspects of connection, but simply to give my best and trust God's Spirit to care for the rest?* (Cue sigh of relief.) Now, I'm all about exchanging controlling expectations for honest needs. As I practice verbalizing my wants, I relieve others from having to play the guessing game. I'm claiming my yeses and nos and trusting others to do the same. Speaking plainly follows Jesus' heart, for in it there are no hidden agendas or passive manipulations, simply "Let your 'Yes' be 'Yes,' and your 'No,' 'No'" (Matthew 5:37 NKJV).

Tension, Assumptions, and Awkward Conversations

Now we dive into the next gooey layer: tension and awkward conversations. *Your mouth's watering and your stomach's churning, isn't it?*

When relationships get weird, I wonder, *Is it me? What did I do?* And those questions can be beautiful, causing me to look inside and change. Sometimes the problem *is* me, and I can respond by softening, listening, and apologizing. And *sometimes* the problem has nothing to do with me. Perhaps my friend is trudging through thick junk and the tension I sense is about *her* and *her* journey. I'll share with you some life-changing words a friend used to encourage me when I was quick to beat myself up: "Maybe," she whispered discerningly, "maybe you get to be Jesus to their hurting heart. Maybe He is using you, not for what you will receive from the relationship, but for the gift of what pursuing their heart will give them. Maybe they are overwhelmed and have nothing extra to offer. Showing up and saying, 'I love you regardless of this tension, and I want you to feel valued while you go through whatever it is you're going through,' may be the beginning of healing and a deeper relationship down the road."

A friend and I shared a moment of tension. The night before, I'd seen her post a picture of her husband and her out to dinner with mutual couple friends. I felt left out because we weren't invited. *Why didn't they think of us? Aren't we fun?* Thoughts swirled on my way to pick up beach towels at her house, and by the time I got there, I was already on the defensive with short responses and a cooler than usual demeanor. Somehow she referenced her meal the night before, and I muttered, "That's not a place we can afford to eat," or something to that effect. And there it was: awkward, slice-it-with-a-knife tension.

My stomach churned. My cheeks flushed. I wondered, *Well, how's this gonna go?* I wanted to run and cross her off my friend list, but if every time a friendship gets awkward I avoid, I'll only know the first level of intimacy, one that easily becomes shallow and stale. *I want deeper,* I decided. She called me when I was on the way home, and I recognized in her emotions that she, too, wanted depth, wanted to push through. She admitted she didn't like how our conversation ended, and then something amazing happened. We pulled out all our insecure assumptions, laid them on the table, and verbalized them—trivial or serious—and allowed each other to shine light as a response.

"I felt embarrassed because we can't afford those types of dinners. I was hurt because you didn't invite us out. Are we not cool enough?" Yes, I felt like a junior higher as I spoke.

Her reply came with tears. "That's not my intent at all, and if anything, I'm trying to be more aware of what pictures I post on social media. Do you think I'm a snob?"

Then, another layer deeper. "I assume"—bad idea, friends—"you don't want to hang out because I have crazy boys who bounce off the walls and your girls are calmer; and when we're together, I wonder if you're evaluating us."

"I actually want to hang out with you and your boys. I didn't think your boys would want to be around younger girls."

Do you see what's going on? Even as I recall our conversation, I laugh at how juvenile it sounds, but it's the truth. It's real. One assumption, one tense conversation holds so much more than a social media post of friends at dinner. To this day, she and I talk about how healing that moment was. When tension and assumption threatened our connection, we chose to see one another's hearts, even through fumbling words, tears, and I-wanna-throw-up anxiety. Communicating value won. At the close of our conversation, we gave each other permission to ask questions when awkward feelings flare, to end growing assumptions before time gives them room to multiply. By valuing our friendship above discomfort, we fought to experience more of Jesus' heart for relationship and gained a trustworthy appreciation in the process.

Man, oh man, though. So often I bomb when it comes to confronting tension. When I first gave communicating value a go, I was petrified. I later told my boys I thought I was going to have diarrhea; my stomach swarmed with bitey moths. *What if I share my heart and she's defensive or angry or thinks I'm lame?* I decided it's more important to be the sincere version of who God created me to be, to speak with honesty and vulnerability, than to offer imitation. And guess what? Those tense conversations didn't go so well. They took practice. They still take practice. Ironically, I'm learning that awkward feelings don't go away with prayers and pondering alone.

One of my errors as I nose dived into awkward territory was neglecting to ask myself what I wanted to communicate and gain from the conversation. Knowing those details before I open my mouth and blubber is helpful. So I led with what I thought was an olive branch but put the tension in another's lap. I led the conversation with, "How do you feel about this?" which caught the other person off guard, unsure of what to say. Three times I did this before I learned, *Oh, I am the one wanting to understand why these tense feelings exist, so I need to lead with my genuine thoughts, as vulnerable and scary as they are.* Now, instead of starting a conversation with "Do you ever notice?" or "Does this feel weird?" I lead with vulnerability: "My feelings are hurt," or "I miss you," or "I'm not sure what happened, but when I see you, I feel a distance and want reconnection, however that looks."

I may fumble and clutch dancing moths inside as I go around and around trying to say what I want to communicate. Eventually, on the fiftieth round, the small door appears, the one marked VALUE, and I open it. "How do you feel valued?" I ask. I listen. Then I share.

Sometimes we agree to forgive and apologize and see each other when it organically happens and expect nothing more. But one thing is for sure—I leave feeling more myself, more brave, more honest. If I want a life full of deep relationships, perhaps I must be the one to lead from deep places first.

What do you need in your relationships? When those weird moments arise, ask yourself, *How can I move through the tension, and what goal do I have stepping forward in this relationship?* It may mean a more intimate friendship, or one of you may choose to sit on the front porch or in the living room. Either way, when we offer truth, then tension, assumptions, and awkwardness no longer weigh the cake down.

From here, it's frosting, friends. Notice the layers? The more we desire real, the more we choose to be genuine in our "sweet spot" relationships. Then the fun part comes, frosting it all with clarifying questions.

Clarifying Questions

A group of us gals was catching up over chai lattes, and one was sharing the same story she'd been sharing for weeks. She was obviously exhausted. Her twin newborns weren't gaining as much as she hoped. She wasn't getting any time with her husband. Everyone was surviving. I could feel my frustration levels shooting through the roof. So I offered a few options that could potentially help her situation—ways we could better support and allow her to get more sleep. The response was crickets.

Later that night I asked myself, *Why do I care so much that there was silence? What am I feeling?* Part of me was identifying a need and trying to offer solutions. Another part of me just wanted to fix her problem. A friend encouraged me to pause and begin with a question. Then I realized, *I didn't even ask.* I was so focused on rescuing her that I neglected to hand her the gift of a clarifying question: *What do you need in this moment? A listening ear? Ideas on how to help your situation? Another chai? A wet nurse and hotel in the Bahamas?* Instead, I bulldozed ahead with solutions.

How can I care without carrying? Am I asking or fixing? Am I offering grace or serving guilt? Am I leading with love or the law? I have to internally whisper these questions when I find myself going into rescue mode.

I do this with God. I feel like I need to bring my resolutions to Him so He'll perform like the gentleman choosing a grand prize waiting behind one of three doors. Except God doesn't need to grant one of my resolutions as a prize. He cares about my heart. The more I choose to respond to my discomfort, bring Him my troubles, ask for His advice, and let myself sit with Him in it, the more I find His Spirit gradually provides the answer. If my faith relationship consisted only of God telling me what to do and offering fix-it strategies, I'd feel more like a robot and less like a friend. Why do I forget to do the same in relationships?

Marriage triggers all sorts of problems and solution-inducing, spicy conversations. Perhaps the most beautiful phrases Bry and I are learning to ask each other when we find our voices raising and wish the other person would just change his or her mind are, "What do you need right now?" "Want me to listen? Encourage?" "Want feedback?" "Do you need a hug?" "How can I help?" It's amazing how grace grows when we give her space to exist without shoving solutions down her pretty throat.

I met a mom at the park near our kids' school. While our young ones ran around the play structure and collected sticks, I listened as she unzipped her story and vulnerably shared. She's on a relationship journey. She is learning who her people are. She is learning who they aren't. After she had her second daughter, now four, she found herself in a postpartum fog, isolating herself from family and friends. "Now that I'm coming out of it, I want people around and am learning how to ask for that." She admitted she was experiencing disappointment with her mom: "I thought she'd be more involved, be excited to be a grandma, but she's sort of just going on with her life. I wanted to be honest, so I called her, and even though it came out messy and she was defensive, she later called me back and told me her side. She noticed me pushing her away, assumed I didn't want a relationship with her, and busied herself with other people. Our relationship has never been stronger because I was honest and told her I missed her, and I was able to hear her story."

I wonder how many relationships can be remedied if I take the time to speak honestly, ask questions, and pray to see hearts.

One friend admitted she gets insecure when too much

time goes by and she hasn't heard from me. "You're on my short list, and if I'm not on yours, that's okay."

As we talk, I ask and listen and understand how to love her specifically. Even if it's a season where I can't hop in the car and connect in person, calling her to let her know I'm thinking of her and wish we could gab over guacamole-doused burritos helps her feel known and secure in our friendship. I don't think this is lame. It's liberating.

As I wrote this book, I communicated all sorts of vulnerabilities to my nest peeps. Especially toward the final countdown, when my inner extrovert screamed for quality time with nearby friends, or even a phone call with those far away, but I had to focus on finishing. So I made a point to call, text, e-mail, write it in the sky. *I need you. I adore you. I just don't want to see your face right now because I have a deadline. But I am thinking of you daily and would totally appreciate encouragement and prayers if I cross your mind.* They actually thanked me. Some admitted they thought I'd died or wondered if I was okay. Communicating value frees us all up to stop assuming and doubting and lets us love each other well.

Real relationships, *real*ationships, resemble the heart of the Father, deep layers of openness, asking, sharing, and mostly listening. I won't nail them perfectly at the first try or ever, but I sure do get more comfortable the more I dig in.

I'm passing you an extra thick slice of Miss Chocolate Layered Cake and giving you a wink. How, friend, how do *you* feel valued?

Grab some forks.

Share.

You can practically taste the decadent sweetness in each layered bite.

LIFE-CHANGING CHOCOLATE CAKE RECIPE

Shared by Garrett Futrell

Cake (for 2 layers)

1½ cups flour

1½ cups sugar

1 cup unsweetened cocoa powder

1½ teaspoons baking soda

1½ teaspoons baking powder

1 teaspoon salt

2 eggs, at room temperature

¾ cup buttermilk

¼ cup plain greek yogurt

½ cup canola oil

1 tablespoon vanilla extract

¾ cup strong brewed coffee, hot

½ cup semisweet chocolate chips (optional)

Whipped Chocolate Buttercream (for 2 layers)

3 sticks (1½ cups) salted butter, softened to room temperature

3 cups powdered sugar

¾ cup unsweetened cocoa powder

2 teaspoons vanilla extract

3–4 tablespoons heavy whipping cream

Cake Instructions:

Preheat oven to 350 degrees.

Grease two 8-inch round cake pans. Line with parchment paper, then butter/spray with cooking spray.

In medium-size bowl, combine flour, sugar, cocoa powder, baking soda, baking powder, and salt. Set aside.

In the bowl of a stand mixer (or use a handheld mixer), beat together eggs, buttermilk, yogurt, oil, and vanilla until smooth.

Slowly add dry ingredients to wet ingredients with mixer on low until there are no longer any clumps of flour. Add coffee and mix until combined. Batter should be pourable but not superthin. Stir in chocolate chips, if using.

Pour batter into cake pans and bake 20 to 25 minutes, until tops are just set and no longer wiggly in center. Remove and let cool 5 minutes, then run knife around edges of pan. Grab two large flat plates, line them with waxed or parchment paper, and invert cakes onto paper-lined plates. Cover and let cakes cool completely before frosting.

Frosting Instructions:

Add butter and powdered sugar to the bowl of a stand mixer (or use a handheld mixer). Beat butter and powdered sugar together until butter is light and fluffy, about 4 minutes. Add cocoa powder and vanilla and beat, scraping down sides as needed another 2 minutes or until there are no streaks of white. Add 3 tablespoons of the heavy cream and whip frosting for 2 to 4 minutes or until light and fluffy. If desired, add the remaining tablespoon of heavy cream (I normally do) and whip until combined. Taste frosting and add more powdered sugar if you like a sweeter or thicker frosting.

Place one layer, flat side up, on plate or cake stand. With knife or offset spatula, spread top with frosting. Place second layer on top, rounded side up, and spread frosting evenly on top and sides of cake. Decorate with sprinkles, chocolate curls, or whatever your heart desires.

9
THANKSGIVING IN MAY

An Invitation to Choose Gratitude

When life is sweet, say thank you and celebrate. And when life is bitter, say thank you and grow.
—Shauna Niequist, *Bittersweet*

It's easy to choose gratitude around a Thanksgiving table. As young kids, we cousins shoved shiny black olives on our fingers and *pop, pop, pop* ate them one by one while the adults heaped turkey and mashed potatoes and that life-changing pretzel Jell-O salad high on plates. If only I could have stolen the bowl of creamed corn and had at it with a ginormous spoon. Now *that* dish is something to be grateful for. Once seated, we went around, each person pausing from bites to share specific reasons they were thankful. It was like a window into their stories, a life layer I wasn't privy to on a regular basis. For many of us, Thanksgiving is the one time a year we hear family or friends intentionally celebrate how blessed we are.

And in a wink, a week's preparation is devoured, china soaks in the sink, the football game is on, and a bunch of full, content bellies sprawl on the couch. *Happy Thanksgiving! Black Friday shopping, anyone?*

Is Thanksgiving a holiday or a lifestyle? I admit, I throw out thanks like Halloween candy when the positive circumstances accumulate. But isn't every single moment an accumulation of my journey? Your journey? Isn't it easy to praise the good and pray away the bad? Isn't life one instance after another, and if the great ones have no hard ones to follow, would we still find thanks? It's like Ralph Waldo Emerson said: "Cultivate the habit of being grateful for every good thing that comes to you, and give thanks continuously. And because all things have contributed to your advancement, you should include all things in your gratitude."[25] Here's where I struggle with thankfulness. I'm not going to jump up and down when horrible things happen to people. I refuse to strap a cheesy grin on my face and say, "God is good. It's *all* good." No, it's not.all.good. Really bad things happen, and when *ick* hits, I'm not about to get out my bubble wand, madly wave it in the sky and declare, "Oh Jesus, I'm so thankful for this crappy situation," and do a double leg kick! That would be a big fat N-O.

I'm learning that thankfulness comes from a space of trust. And I can't be thankful when my life is overflowing with excess, because then I focus on the stuff, instead of the stuff giver. While contentment reflects a grateful heart, comparison produces a heart focused on what's lacking instead of what *is*. My spirit of gratitude comes when I stop looking around and wondering, *When is my life going to get better or become something special?* How un.grate.ful. What I'm really saying is, *God, this isn't quite good enough for the story I'm wanting.*

A naive newlywed, I knew little of the maturity needed to appreciate perseverance and delayed gratification. On a downtown date, we passed a storefront, admired the rich blues and patterned textures of seasonal pillows in the window, and off-the-cuff I hinted, "I just *love* those pillows," expecting my new husband to march right into that home store and purchase said pillows. "I'll take four for my wife. Because she *loves* them. And *needs* them."

But he didn't.

"Cool," he said with a nod, and on we walked. The longer I walked, the more I steamed. "Umm, why aren't we getting those pillows?" I asked. "Don't you *love* me?" (Yes, I literally uttered those shallow words.)

"Because we have pillows at home, and every time we see something new, it doesn't necessarily mean we have to buy it." (Cue pouting wife.) I'm embarrassed to admit it, but it's true. You know why I remember that story? Because in a world of so many *yeses*, I heard a *no*. And it stuck. And I detested the no. But my husband's wisdom taught me to lean into delayed gratification because I appreciate it more in the long run.

When we moved into our first home, we saved every penny for a statement couch. I worked extra events at the winery, and Bry robbed banks (kidding) to stockpile for a huge sectional couch. I knew the one—a cushy dream of an L-shaped space large enough to seat five couples for an evening gathering. It was cozy and a greenish blue, like the crest of a wave after a huge storm. For a season our living room sat naked, until the day we poured all our pennies together to order the couch. And when it was delivered, I jumped on every section, claiming home in the corner. I probably slept there the first night. It was just a couch, but it symbolized time and trust and patience. For years it seated nursing moms and couples and crying friends. It was the backdrop for marital arguments and tender makeups and couch dates. I'd never been so thankful to plop my bum on something saved and sacrificed for and much awaited. I was all the more grateful because it hadn't been acquired instantaneously but over time.

Then I became a mom and found myself wanting, never satisfied. I spent the first couple of years literally changing diapers but mentally in a new town or on a tropical island or at a job where I spoke with adults all day. I was nowhere near present, and comparison shrouded any chance for contentment. Looking back, I wish I would have been honest with my longings and taken my disappointments and expectations for first-time-mom life to God, but I fed the beast. I numbed out on social media. I idealized my former life and planned our future. So many sweet in-the-present moments I missed out on.

God, though, in His graciousness didn't waste one moment. He allowed me to gather discontented thoughts, but He seasoned them with clarity. Eventually, a clear picture of what it means to embrace a spirit of gratitude came into focus, one of choosing to emulate God's own heart. I found that fullness and life and the source of all joy is found in spending time with Him, drawing from Him, then reflecting His Son.

God stripped me of excess as we went from a two-income family down to one salary, and given quiet hours alone at home with a new muncher, He invited perspective. Budgets were tight and the stress palpable. One morning, I walked into the kitchen to see Bryan sitting at our worn table, defeated, staring at an open computer, crying. "It's so tight," he said. "I don't know how we're going to pay our mortgage this month. We're five hundred dollars and fifty cents short." Gone were the days of going out to dinner and buying whatever cute top would only get lost days later in a full closet. My brain went into problem-solving mode. Maybe I could work an event at the winery or grab a catering gig or see if someone needed help managing *something*. I scrambled to organize who could watch Tanner so I could contribute, and an overwhelming sense of anxiety hovered as I realized we had no family close by to help. Holding tiny Tanner in our grass-green kitchen, lit by dawn's glow, I pulled my boys close, and we prayed as never before. "God, please take care of us. Do a miracle."

Two weeks later a check arrived in our mailbox, a forgotten tax return in the exact amount due for that month's mortgage. It was the first time "those stories out there" became "our story right here." Of a Father who loves to give gifts and hears His kids' cries.

A lesson in thankfulness isn't one learned overnight but gradually. When I emerged from the baby zone, I was able to recognize that I'd been in a mama fog and admit, *Maybe the infant stage wasn't my sweet spot, and maybe there are other moms for whom it's not either. How is God going to use my story to encourage women to soak up simple, thankworthy moments? If I'm not grateful in the small things, how in the world will I be thankful in the big things?*

God loves giving good gifts to His kids, and He does so in abundance and often. Unfortunately, I didn't see them because I was looking for them in the wrong places—in the past or the future—instead of smack-dab in front of me. *Well, hello, entitled heart, aren't you a bit too greedy for your britches? How about appreciating the life laid before you, the one you chose, even though it comes with surprises along the way?*

If everything I want comes my direction, I'll never have to learn how to be grateful, because gratitude is learned by being thankful for what is, not obsessing over what is not. Until I am satisfied with the Giver, all the pillows and couches and lip gloss bouquets in the world won't create an appreciative spirit. Okay fine, it would make my heart happy for a week, but then new pillows would mock from a store window, lip gloss would run out, and my couch would get stained, and then what?

Isn't it our tendency to celebrate the tangible gifts, to be thankful for what we can hold in our hands? The lessons I'm learning in waiting? God loves me and wants me to be content *in* Him, *with* Him. With that understanding comes a renewed awareness, for I.am.blessed. Every good thing comes from Him. The trials and mundane moments that seem like they lack a specific calling? Those are invitations to experience His heart and cultivate a thankful spirit, and as Margaret Feinberg says in her book *Organic God*, "When you focus more on what is being taken from you than what has already been given, you'll quickly lose the wonder that comes with giving."[26] I don't know about you, but celebrating Thanksgiving once a year is not enough. It's almost like we need another gratitude celebration at the halfway point before the next Thanksgiving.

A few years ago, at the close of November, I looked at the calendar and babbled aloud to Bry, "What if we create a new tradition surrounding thankfulness, an evening where we invite a few couples for drinks and appetizers and sit under the back patio lights and communally celebrate and praise God? What if we intentionally create space to share about our current seasons in work, marriage, parenting, whatever? What if Thanksgiving doesn't have to just happen in November but can also happen on a spring night in May? Like a *Thanksgiving in May*?"

I noted Bryan's reaction and visualized his wheels turning, too! "Let's do it," he grinned.

Spring came, and with it, the calendar's turn to May.

Invitations went out, and the first annual Thanksgiving in May evening was upon us. Our hope was for an intimate setting, one where people felt safe sharing, with no need to hurry. A night simply to be, to celebrate and nibble and sip, to honor sacred stories of God moving in real people in real time.

Since no party is complete without food, each couple brought an appetizer, and on small plates we cozied toasted bruschetta bites, spicy sausage paired with sauces, various cheeses, Brie topped with cranberries and apples and baked in a puff pastry, and dessert. Because *dessert*.

We clinked glasses, and on paint-peeled chairs and weathered patio benches we circled around the crackling fire pit. Near the backyard patio slider leaned the boys' bunk bed ladder, which served as an upcycled blanket shelf for outdoor gatherings such as these.

I was so excited I could burst. "Thank you for coming," I beamed. "This idea has been one I've been thinking about for a while, and who better to begin this tradition with than you? The heart behind this really is to just come together as friends, as chosen family, to practice thankfulness for whatever is happening in our lives right now. The good, the bad, the ugly. I believe something sacred happens when we utter gratitude as a group, especially for the areas that aren't exactly easy or thanksgiving worthy."

It could have flopped. People could have kindly piled a plate, enjoyed a glass of wine, and excused themselves to relieve a babysitter. However, that first Thanksgiving in May, every soul verbalized thankfulness, their faces aglow from fire pit flames. When the heat died down, Bryan threw more logs on, sending ashy gusts of black smoke blowing in all directions, and couples were forced to play musical chairs as they scooted to the left or right, depending on which direction the breeze blew. It was real life. A backyard setting. Twinkly lights and orange blossom air. Trusted friends. Thankful hearts. And the occasional wind change bringing fire pit debris.

One person shared about his new job and a quick promotion, which helped with the raised rent. "I'm thankful for a God who provides for me so I can provide for my family."

"I'm thankful for my kids even though they drive me crazy. They force me to focus on where my time is best spent."

Sweet seasons. Challenging seasons. We piled gratitude stories one on top of the other, almost as fuel for the flames, sending praise straight to heaven. Then Garrett would throw in a funny story, and Em would refill her glass, and Britt would throw a blanket over her bare knees, and we'd circle back to purposeful praise. For hope despite death and for clear cancer scans. For fulfilled dreams and for new life out of devastation. For improving family dynamics and for deepening friendships.

I believe God smiles when we take the time to sit in His presence and thank Him for doing life with us. I believe the angels lend an ear when we gather in groups and communally give thanks. It doesn't have to look a certain way or follow a rigid practice. Thanksgiving doesn't have to happen in November or May. Thanksgiving *every day* is God's desire, because every day there is something worth being grateful for. And when we verbalize it from mouth to air, it gathers and gains traction and becomes this invisible force that echoes, "God is good and worthy to be praised."

Thanksgiving happens when normal folks like us declare praises like Paul instructed in 1 Thessalonians 5:16–18: "Rejoice always, pray continually, give thanks in all circumstances; for this is God's will for you in Christ Jesus." It's no mistake that *rejoicing*, *praying*, and *thanking* done *always*, *continually*, and *in all circumstances* creates who God wants you and me to be. If this is His will for us, He obviously cares about encouraging His children to live joyfully and fully and with thanksgiving on our tongues. When we choose appreciative awareness for the small things, we live contentedly and are quick to praise for the big things.

Please hold. How many times have we asked the question, "What's God's will for my life? Please, Lord, just write it with lipstick on my bathroom mirror." But did you catch this? God's will for our lives is to give thanks in all circumstances. Always. No matter what. Even when life stinks. (Deep breath in.)

And if we look closer in response, what do those three tasks—praying, rejoicing, and giving thanks—have in common? They are all something we offer back to God, part of our ongoing conversation—a continuous listen and share and share and listen relationship—as He so generously places His will in our laps. And His will is to choose to see Him as the Giver and to offer thanksgiving continuously. His will has to do with keeping Him at the center of our thoughts, our dreams, our actions. When we pray, rejoice, and give thanks, there aren't any gooey feelings or a mustering up of nice, soft words. It's not ignoring hurt or shoving the pain of lame circumstances aside. Illness and changed plans and harsh words can be paralyzing. Should we flash our pearly whites, clap our hands, invite the church ladies for a buffet, and sing, "Let's praise Jesus, whoop de whoop"? No, there's nothing genuine about artificial thanks. If my nearest and dearest can spot my phoniness, why do I think I can fool God? He wants my praise, but He wants the real kind. When I see His heart in whatever the day holds, believe it's His best for me, and respond with gratitude—that, I'm learning, is true thanksgiving.

When we worship together like we did on the first annual Thanksgiving in May, laughing about listening to squabbly kids, acknowledging the fear of not being enough, avoiding fire pit gusts, we claim faith even when we don't feel it, for we can see God's work through others' eyes. Through the filter of a genuine Jesus. Before my dad's death, I said thanks for the shiny parts of life, the areas that molded to my ideal plan, and now I wholeheartedly welcome it all. There will be good and bad, and I will give praise for it, and God will be glorified in it. Even when shrouded in smoke.

Being thankful is a choice, and living gratefully, a natural response to a full, appreciative heart. If Ann Voskamp can utter poetic thanks for the detailed colors in the arc of a bubble while doing dishes in *One Thousand Gifts*, I can certainly choose to find minuscule details to cherish each day, as well. When I respond to a moment, like my boys waving for me to watch a family of ducks play in the wash below, cupping it carefully with awe, I can better see God fingerprints on it. For up close is where I notice details. The creativity. The invitation to thank the Maker for blowing my mind with a confetti of gifts, regardless of whether they are covered in black fire pit debris.

During a recent Honeymoon Friday, Bry and I biked over to our local secondhand store, which has an awesome book section. I could browse for hours, and sometimes do, in search of a pair of jeans to replace Tanner's holey ones or to snag school backpacks or stroll the aisles noting, "What's one's junk is truly another's treasure." It was here I discovered a tattered copy of Mitch Albom's *Tuesdays with Morrie*. An endearing, clever read, the book is about the relationship between a former professor, Morrie, living out his final months on earth and his previous student who visits him on a weekly basis. The young money-hungry sportswriter sits for hours with Morrie in his home and continues his visits throughout Morrie's gradual deterioration. He notes Morrie's appreciation for life. For people. For sharing. For listening and admiring outdoor birds' whistling. Coming to one's end invites bitterness or thankfulness, and Morrie chooses thankfulness. It's one of my favorite reads for the simple thought-provoking nuggets toward grateful living.

At the hint of the next spring, air once again fragrant with orange blossoms and freesia, I was already planning the second annual Thanksgiving in May when Li'l Mom called. She was having a grief-stricken day, those days fewer now that it had been two years since my dad's passing, but ache still accompanying when struck.

She'd been eating lunch at her outdoor bistro table in the backyard, a gray day matching her mood, and as she thought about her "Pooder," loss waves hit her with full force. Through her tears she noticed how the charcoal skies parted and lemony rays shone across the yard on an old liquidambar tree, bare and naked from winter months. It stilled her to stare longer. She noticed several branches shooting tender green foliage and leaned over her lunch for a closer look, and tears came. Suddenly one bird, then two, then three flew in to perch and twitter. She told me later the Holy Spirit spoke to her about how she was like that tree—sorrowful and empty, having nothing to give. But because of His faithfulness, she would bloom again; her life would provide shade and protection, safety and beauty.

As she sobbed into the phone and relayed the story, she said, "That tree is like me. I lost my Dean. I felt stripped and bare. But now that tree is growing back stronger. Once again it will offer shade." And here is where her words touched me deeply. "I want to be like that tree, Bekah. I want God to use my bare situation, one that was and is painful, to offer shade to others. I want birds to take refuge in my shade. To feel safe and protected. I want to be like that tree."

I sat in her words and allowed them to float around until I responded. "You *are* that tree, Mom. God is using you every day. Even in the days you still feel nubby and bare and without leaves, your gratitude for life stirs others to find thanks, too." I'm not sure thanks is authentic if offered when life mainly sails smooth. If I'm honest, my prayers used to consist of *God, please keep my boys safe and everyone healthy, and can You please be with us?* What does that even mean? Being thankful shouldn't be my pathetic cry to avoid hardships. Real gratitude says thank you when winter comes and leaves are blown and you're standing bare and cold and vulnerable and even when shaking, commit: "I am thankful in all circumstances and will celebrate nonetheless."

How can we celebrate a genuine faith relationship if we don't give thanks in the bare seasons as well as in the abundant ones? How do we live with thankful overflow to pour on those who matter around us? How do we say thank you in authentic ways?

After we hung up, I found my mom's verse about the tree and the leaves in Psalm 1:3—"That person is like a tree planted by streams of water, which yields its fruit in season and whose leaf does not wither—whatever they do prospers"—and I knew this year's Thanksgiving in May would be different, a sixty-fifth birthday celebration for Li'l Mom, an evening to thank God for how He used her faithfulness in so many ladies' lives.

On May 28, Li'l Mom's nearest and dearest gathered at the Pogue Cottage for a birthday version of Thanksgiving in May, an evening to honor and intentionally give thanks for her life. Bubbles and brownies and magenta and gold décor welcomed her as the guest of honor. Vibrant pom-pom yarn swung from the top of the window along the ceiling and reached to the other end of the room like a cheery circus tent. Li'l Mom, with a glass of champagne in one hand and chocolate in the other, sat in an oversize comfy chair, and with friends circled around her, I shared the heartbeat behind her birthday soiree, ending with the tree story. Then I invited her friends, her "birds," to shower her with thanks for how she offered them shade. On our rustic coffee table sat a blue bucket holding bare branches sprouting tall, and nestled near, a small bowl held paper leaves. "Will you write one word of affirmation for how Mom embodies the story of the protective tree?" I asked her friends. "How has God used her in your life? Why are you thankful for her?" One by one each lady penned a gold leaf, and the once bare branches shimmered with celebratory words.

How is God's Spirit inviting you to practice gratitude? What stirs within as you think about creating your own Thanksgiving in May? Where do you feel bare, having no energy to offer thanks? What prompts you to shout thanks from the rooftops? The response is yours, but let me ask you this: Do you want to live content with what *is* or bitter at what is *not yet*? How are you choosing a grateful spirit not only in November but also in the other months? Where are you noticing and how are you responding to the smoke and bare branches and bright green leaves? Where is frustration crowding in when a thankful heart may be the very act to free you toward a full life? Where you feel like pouting, where is He inviting praise?

When I choose to celebrate God's goodness *always*, *continually*, and *in all circumstances*, gratitude is embodied, even if blocked by ashy smoke or cut down by bare branches. Will I utter thanks before the debris clears and leaves grow back? Anticipating Real as the source?

Of light.

Of strength.

A safe place to find warmth and shade.

To which I hold my glass to the twinkly sky and cheer, "Thank You."

10
GODSENSE

An Invitation to Sharpen Our Five Fabulous Senses

If a man is to live, he must be all alive, body, soul, mind, heart, spirit.

—Thomas Merton, *Thoughts in Solitude*

*D*rumroll, please. Ladies and gentlemen, God has officially left the box. The precious, infant-sized, bland cardboard box. And I'm not about to shove Him back in, for I've been wrecked in the best way—with GODsense, a sudden appreciation and insatiable desire to see, taste, smell, hear, feel Him in every moment of every day.

Has she gone crazy? you may wonder. *Is she overspiritualizing?* I'll let you decide, but I will warn you: where before I experienced life at the surface, it's now ultradimensional, rich, flavorful, intoxicatingly vibrant, and multifaceted. GODsense, my friend, is nowhere near boring.

GODsense changes my perspective from once living as though sensory situations happened *to me* to now living *into* senses, gobbling up each one as a willing, all-in participant. With a tilt-my-head-back eagerness to embrace however God is offering Himself. For there is sacred work in noticing. . .in offering attention to everyday details and, once exposed, craving them in never-before ways with an all-sensory appetite for smells, sights, sounds, tastes, and textures.

On our handmade backyard swing, cool air slowly pushed me forward near the kitchen slider then back toward our neighbor's orange tree peeking over the trumpet-vined wall. Underneath, Bruiser napped, as classical melodies wafted from our cottage. Orange blossoms, a touch of salt air, and the smell of fresh-dug earth greeted every sway. Nearby, a bowl of homemade trail mix brought childhood memories flooding as I scooped handfuls of almonds, raisins, and an occasional M&M with a crunching and mixing of flavors. This, my friend, is GODsense, a manifestation of how God uses our simple senses to reflect His personal and creative nature. And it has rocked my world. Never will I be able to eat a peach without looking for the door in the pit, hear a song without placing it with a memory, or smell a family of eucalyptus trees without bowing under their fragrant leaves, knowing God smiles as they salute in the palm of His hand.

Remember when I shared about how life shifted into sharp focus days after Dad's loss? About how I suddenly had nothing to give anyone and was forced to just be? *Yeah, that was fun.* What caused such an irreversible transformation was how gracious God was in that season, because let's be honest, there was no jumping out of bed to grab my Bible. No scheduled quiet times or worship sessions were happening. Only taking initial steps toward an understanding that God gets it. He knows me. And He knows you. He knows what's going on in our lives, and He is meeting us exactly where we are in such personal, out-of-the-box displays. This is where fresh perspective completely came out of left field. Something unexpected occurred; every sense—taste, touch, sound, smell, and sight—was heightened.

Why haven't I experienced life like this before? I wondered. Have you muttered similar words? Or maybe you connect to when I used to beg God, "Please, for the love, just talk to me. Just show me. Just meet me in my stuff. Hello.out.there?"

I'd believed in Jesus most of my life, but this? This was new. This was truly living! Apparently the box I'd put God in—a safe, sturdy, boring box—was not going to suffice, and that suited me just fine, because *safe* and *boring* are no longer adjectives I want to label the Creator of the world.

When I first noticed GODsense at work, I simultaneously became aware of the typical ways I experienced God prior to "the box has blown up" days. Looking back, I saw how most of my Christian experiences were focused on connecting with my Creator through the sense of sight. Coastal sunsets and wildflower sprays and romping puppies whispered of His creativity. And as God Himself said in Genesis, after throwing out oceans and penning His name in the sky and dotting it with stars, "It's good."

But now that the darn box had detonated, my whole being couldn't neglect to acknowledge GODsense in a million humble facets, and it was more than I could process. Bry would come home from work, and I'd chatter about exploring a local park with the boys, scents of eucalyptus trees, various shades of green, crisp apple snacks, crunchy leaves tap dancing in the air. He'd look at me under his dark eyelashes and smile.

He caught on.

The boys caught on.

GODsense does that. Once you experience His Spirit inviting you to notice and respond and celebrate Him in all of it, you can't ignore how real He is.

I wonder if this is true for most of us. Do we unintentionally participate with the Divine through limited senses? I did. Other than observing His reflection in beach waves or visual gifts, I didn't know any different. Do those with a bent toward the visual—like photographers and designers—experience God mostly through sight? Do they also get goose bumps at hearing crickets chirp and babies giggle? Do musicians, their gifting toward hearing melodies, pause to worship at the smell of a redwood forest, pines fresh and trunks earthy? Are food critics—their palates trained to appreciate subtle notes of cherry, paprika, or smoked salt—stilled by buttery cotton sheets and warm pajamas hot out of the dryer?

If we don't live with GODsense, I believe it's not for lack of desire but for untapped awareness. Before my dad passed, I would say, "I want to soak up every part of who Jesus is," and I meant it. I simply wasn't aware there were more avenues to know Him beyond seeing His handiwork, listening to worship music, or reading my Bible.

And so my senses came alive. Some may call it overspiritualizing, but I call it a miracle.

Taste

Foods taste richer, sweeter, and more complexly simple; savory grilled tri-tip melts like butter with each bite; salad heaped with crumbly feta, firm cherry tomatoes, shiny bell peppers, and toasted pine nuts explodes a combination of creaminess and crunch. Chilled iced tea, glasses rimmed with a generous lemon wedge, washes down salty garlic bread during a summer evening barbeque.

Are you like me and *uhh-sessed* with the Food Network?

I mean come on. Where do they get the inspiration for combining such crazy flavors? Whoever thought of marrying chili and coffee or squirting a spritz of lime on a smiling papaya? Who was the first person to utter, "You know what would be life changing? Smooshing peanut butter and chocolate together!" Whoever it was, bless them. Pretty sure on the eighth day, that was the good Lord's idea.

We are a foodie family, our teamwork made up of my hubby who cooks, while I bake. Bryan's been warned if he ever died, he'd kill the three of us in one fell swoop because we'd live off of brownies for dinner. So I guess when I say I bake, I mean desserts. And by desserts, I'm talking chocolate. While I'll never turn down an incredible entrée, I'll order two sweets in place of any meal. Desserts like gooey cookie dough topped with a generous scoop of vanilla bean ice cream. Or oatmeal chocolate chip cookies. Or bread pudding lathered in a toffee downpour, topped with a thick whipped cream dollop. Or fudgy, decadent cake. Clearly I have a problem. But seriously, thank God for cake. You do know, it was His idea. The dessert genius spoke of it in Numbers 11:7–8 when He described how to make it with manna by gathering it, grinding it, boiling it, and making cakes with it. *Yes, Lord, I will do just that.* Regularly, my barefoot boys sit on the counter carefully cracking eggs and spooning flour into a shiny mixing bowl. They help stir and lick and stir and taste, and our time together creates a nonfussy way to talk about how God makes all of the ingredients and flavors and how He loves it when we enjoy ourselves through our sense of taste.

When Tanner was two, the Christmas cookie tradition began with Mana, Bryan's mom. Side by side, Tanner on his step stool and Mana in her apron, the duo mixed and rolled and baked cookies. Some years they decorated upside down gingerbread heads to resemble Rudolph; some years they dipped Oreos in a bath of dark chocolate then dunked them in crushed peppermint to dry on her kitchen island—only to devour most of them an hour later. As soon as Ty was old enough for his own step stool, he, too, donned an apron and joined the cookie tradition. As they measured and licked frosting from fingers, they not only spent quality time together as grandsons and Grandma, they enjoyed GODsense through taste. And when they turned their backs, I'm sure God's Spirit was right there, scooping a finger into the bowl of warm, rich chocolate.

Appreciating intricate flavors, spices, and foods has become an avenue to worship the flavor Creator for His wild imagination. Taste invitations don't get more average than breakfast, lunch, or dinner, and whether it's pouring cereal and crunching on *snap, crackle, pop* krispies or tasting parts of our garden in a dinner salad, every bite becomes a way to experience God's good gifts to us in the normal offerings of a meal.

Tanner experienced GODsense when we read Roald Dahl's *James and the Giant Peach* together. At the story's beginning, the peach grew to a ginormous size, and James entered inside the fruit's juicy flesh and found himself at the pit, where a tiny door welcomed him to meet an abode of life-size insects. Since then every peach-eating experience we enjoy is made complete by attempting to find "a door" in the creviced pit. For in enjoying a simple peach, another surprise awaits in the form of a pit. Just as God says in Genesis 1:29, "I give you every seed-bearing plant on the face of the whole earth and every tree that has fruit with seed in it. They will be yours for food." See? God even meets us in the produce section, with fruit. With a story about a boy and a giant peach. With a seed. If you want God to be real to your kids, help them look for Him in the smallest of ways. There are seeds everywhere. You just have to plant them, watch them grow, pick from them, and look close for the door.

Touch

Touching feet to bike pedals and heels to hills feels purposeful. As do hands wrapped around my boys' smaller ones, and the safe weight of Bry's hugging the back of my neck. How beautiful that God gave us the sense of touch. He didn't create blobs, but beings who *need*, *crave*, *thrive from* touch. Whether it's feeling a warm hand, experiencing a hug, making love, we are reminded of our humanity, of our desire for intimacy with our Father.

A passage surrounding touch that moves me to tears is the one found in Mark 8:22–25. Imagine watching a blind man being led outside the village and Jesus putting spit on his eyes and laying His hands on him. Lean closer. Do you hear Jesus ask, "Do you see anything?" The once blind man says, "I see people; they look like trees walking around." Again Jesus puts his hand on the man's eyes. At once the man's sight is completely restored and "he [sees] everything clearly." Wow. What stirs me at reading this account is how Jesus "put his hands" on the man. Counselors say that when people hurt, connection as simple as a gentle hand on a shoulder can be life giving. Think of a time when you were sad or afraid and a friend offered a hug. Touch is powerful; physical gestures speak to our souls, in a moment, reaching out can transcend words.

My college roommate, Ber, was a neonatal intensive care unit nurse for thirteen years and has shared a dozen stories about the power of touch in the form of kangaroo care, skin to skin with fragile babe and mama. Babies whose lives are at risk show miraculous progress in heart strength, oxygen levels, and weight gain. Humans have a wondrous innate need to experience touch. Perhaps it's a tiny reflection of the way God longs to hold us as His children.

Adventures involving GODsense through touch took on a whole new meaning for our family. Bike rides became a spiritual experience. Family hikes, the boys leading with sticks and collecting stray golf balls at Crystal Cove Beach, were a thrill.

And when Tanner admitted, "I don't believe in God," we were able to point him to the sense of touch, to the wind. "Do you feel the air's breeze? And your warm blankets and our big family squeezes? God is in those little things, showing Himself to you. Sometimes He uses hugs and wind and blankets, and other times He reaches within and holds your heart."

Whether you run cross-country or wipe runny noses or dig gardens or type words, imagine God smiling as you sense Him in those simple tasks of touch.

Sound

What immediately comes to mind when you think of sound? Music, right? I adore how melodies and tunes and instruments become the pattern of life, heard awake and in dreams when asleep; how I note worship music in the background while strolling a local store, James Taylor's familiar voice in a grocery aisle; how brothers come running every time "Sugar Pie, Honey Bunch" belts from our iPod playlist, our family song beckoning them to jump into my arms, their energetic legs wrapped around my waist as we whip and nae nae in the kitchen.

And then there was God's Spirit voice ever present, a sound I hadn't known like I do now. I'm discovering how gentle Jesus is. Not a yeller, He whispers in the waves, breezes, rain. Before my senses were awakened, I'd ask, "What does God's voice sound like?" Now I pause, attune my ears, and there He is. "Call to me and I will answer you and tell you great and unsearchable things you do not know" (Jeremiah 33:3). Why do I expect the Almighty to talk in a low rumble when He is not confined to words alone but uses the sea and seagulls and sand to echo His presence through crashes, cries, and crunching underfoot? The question isn't "What does His voice sound like?" but "Am I creating space to hear Him?" Or, as Margaret Feinberg says, "Listening to God's voice requires more than just my ears; it requires my eyes, my mind, my spirit, my entire being to recognize the God-nudges in life."[27] What I love about the Spirit's voice is how He speaks truth, words that don't come from little. ol'.me. When I sense a hidden gem within, recognizing it as His voice, John 6:63 reminds me: "The Spirit gives life; the flesh counts for nothing. The words I have spoken to you—they are full of the Spirit and life." When Ty turned three, his little will tested ours hourly—wait, by the minute. I'd laugh and say, "He keeps us on our toes *and* our knees," but I wasn't kidding. I was voracious to love him even when I didn't like him. One day I called Bry, beyond done. Yelling, reacting, crying. You name it, we'd been through it that day, and I felt at a loss, like a complete failure. I had no idea how to best love our boy and that night fell asleep with a heavy heart. At 2:00 a.m. I woke, and as I made my way to our bathroom, I heard what can only be God's creative voice, because especially on that day, I couldn't have come up with those words on my own. *"Ty is your child who is going to push every.single.button to see how you'll react. Love him,"* came gentle words. *"Just.love.him."*

Love him. Love him. Love him.

In the dark, I broke, my face in my hands, and nodded in silence. How did God know to offer me an answer before I even asked for His perspective? Yet He did. He *does*. Isaiah 65:24 says, "Before they call I will answer; while they are still speaking I will hear." What an amazing visual of God listening and responding. Here I was complaining about our boy, and God woke me up to speak encouragement with specific ways for how to best love our Ty.

Do you, too, wonder about what God's voice sounds like? Have you prayed to hear Him? In a worship song? A family jingle? A beach walk? The voice of His Spirit on how to parent your child? He will answer when you ask. And most likely it will be more amazing and unexpected than ordinary words.

Smell

Smells explode at every turn. Fragrance overwhelms in roses, jasmine, and freesia tucked in rich, damp dirt, creating a backyard celebration of flowers and earth. Chocolate aromas float from the oven, and sea salt carries from the beach along wispy clouds, chasing us as we play in the front yard.

In creating our senses, God spared no details, and with smell, He went above and beyond. When He could simply dip roses in clouds and fling them through sunsets, He didn't pause there but poured fragrant perfume on each petal.

Do you find that your sharpest memories are associated with the sense of smell? Perfume from your wedding day, fall candles, a dish your mom prepared growing up—the one that if you re-create it in your own kitchen instantly transports you to your childhood table? What smells carry stories from a distinct moment in time?

When I was little, I adored giving my mom's mom a make-over. Grandma, sitting on the living room floor, smoothed her dress with her petite hands and then leaned those hands behind her, lifted her face, eyes closed to the bright afternoon light, and allowed me to get lost in her makeup drawer. For hours I painted her thin eyelids with blue chalky shadow, then circled her brush in the blush talc canister, pulling every pink particle from its sides to dab on her linen cheeks. And her coral lipstick. I can still smell the waxy, tart fragrance as I drew her thin lips, trying to keep in line as she shared stories, talking well into the late afternoon shadows.

Smells are a gift reopened long after their scent disappears.

I have other scented GODsense memories, like Chantilly bubble bath in Li'l Mom's huge tub, where, as a junior higher, I'd escape with a good book and cozy myself in floral encased bubbles. Or visiting Grandma and Grandpa Harris's home in Fallbrook and breathing in the crisp, sawdusty scent of wood curls from Grandpa's shed where he carved eagles and robins, mixed with the burnt smell his detailing instrument made as fragile tan shavings fell like feathers to the floor.

Scents are like heaven's gift. And the most touching gift came in a legacy journal my mom discovered when cleaning out Dad's classroom. When she brought the treasure to my house, it's as though I knew I was supposed to read my dad's words outside in nature, a place alive with scents and textures and space.

"We're going to Pirate Park," I told the boys. They grabbed their swords, and I, a blanket, water, and the legacy journal. And while they searched for treasure, zigzagging their ways through a labyrinth of shoulder-high bushes, I sat under a canopy of eucalyptus trees and opened to page 1.

> *What did you enjoy doing most as a child?*
> Dad's response: *I remember the grand adventure of growing up in a small town. Everywhere you looked, you could find open space or groves of orange trees. I was much like Tom Sawyer, and each and every day was a new and grand adventure.*
>
> *What was your favorite childhood room?*
> Dad's response: *My favorite was our big family room that had a huge brick fireplace. I remember watching that blazing fire with huge stumps of eucalyptus.*

How can we experience a spiritual moment with our senses? Beyond simply smelling—how can we find deeper faith through a God who wants to connect with us through perfume or herbs?

Marlyn is my chosen grandma and the first woman to pique my interest in all things perfumey. As a young girl, I remember darting from Sunday school to grab a doughnut at the welcome center as I made my way to my parents' classroom. On the path, I looked for Marlyn's hug. Her delicious, fragrant hug. "You smell amazing," I told her. "Tea rose," she said with a wink. In junior high, she gifted me a delicate bottle, and on my bathroom counter it sat, making me feel quite mature and fancy. And Marlyn-ish.

Now decades later, Marlyn still carries a sweet-smelling presence about her, and when we gather as the Fab Five—my mom, godsister, godmom, "Grandma" Marlyn, and me—at some point I ask her, "What are you wearing these days?" And then I sit as close as I possibly can without taking up residence on her lap.

During one of our gatherings at a Mariposa restaurant, we were finishing our lunch of chicken salad and mandarin orange soufflé, *cheers*ing champagne flutes and savoring sweet stories, when we noticed a private patio event hosted by a well-known perfume designer. We asked our waitress, because after an afternoon of serving our crazy crew, she was now our new BFF, "What's going on out there? You think you can snag some samples for us?" we joked. Well, she did better than that. Suddenly a striking marketing rep joined our party to give us a private showing of the London-based perfume's spring collection, focused on herbs. She explained how the perfume designer hoped to use the best quality ingredients for that time, and when the limited line was gone, the next seasonal collection would be released.

"You're all about using what's available in the present," I gushed. *Brilliant*. The rep, clearly passionate about her career, spritzed and passed samples around our circular table—Wild Strawberry and Parsley, Sorrel and Lemon Thyme, Nasturtium and Clover—as each of us closed our eyes and drew generous inhales. When Carrot Blossom and Fennel landed under Marlyn's nose, I watched her eyelids shut then pop open as she beamed, "This is Don. This is exactly how Don smells." Marlyn invited our new perfume friend into her story and shared about her hubby, Don, a retired farmer. "I always knew what part of the farm he'd been working in that day. And this"—she paused and waved the carrot blossom fragrance around—"this is how he smelled after working in the carrot crop." When the Lavender and Coriander herb blend made its way to Marlyn, she grinned again. "Mmm. Lavender. This smells like him, too." Something about watching her expression and knowing a fragrance encompassed Marlyn's sweet Don brought an emotional lump to my throat. If we could all bottle up the smell of those we hold dear, can you imagine?

After lunch, the Fab Five made our way downstairs to the perfume counter, and Marlyn purchased the limited herb garden collection. I can't help but smile as I imagine her wearing her farmer hubby's scent as she runs errands, plays with her great-grandchildren, and brunches with her husband of sixty-two years. Memories of their young days as a farming family, sweet soil and lingering scents of carrot blossom, parsley, and thyme, bring them back to where they first started. How could I think God is boring to create scents echoing of memories and love and the toil of earth where He first uttered creation into existence? Give me carrot blossoms any day, in the form of a Marlyn hug and her sweet Don scent.

As I pored over my dad's legacy journal, I came to this prompt: *What kind of outdoor work do you enjoy?* and my dad's response: *A weekend is not complete without some time in the yard—either mowing, trimming, working with plants, or just plain vegging in God's creation. Laurie and I have always enjoyed planting roses, tending roses, and of course sharing them with others. God, You are amazing that a perfume can come from Your works. . .sheer beauty and majesty from one touch of Your hand.*

By noticing delicate fragrances of flowers, ocean air scents, and perfume, I glimpse a window into how our Father must smell, as I make myself at home by His side or in His lap. How rich to breathe in the smells surrounding our days and invite my kids to recognize Him with their own sniffers. *Do you smell that? It's the smell of the Father.*

Sight

With GODsense, I experience textures, shapes, and design elements at work in nature. Sunset colors melt into sherbet hues of purple and pink dripping into warm oranges and yellows as they create an ombré art-on-sky canvas of vivid to pale shades. Our cottage décor is inspired by elements from outdoors—sea glass, metals, and peacock plumes.

Studies show that "83 percent of the information people retain is received visually."[28] In doing so, we experience spiritual stirrings through what we see. It's for this reason Tanner and Ty tug my arm with squeals of "Mom, come look at the clouds." Something is deposited into our beings from the beginning of time that draws us to a stunning sunset or body of water, features that echo an even greater source of visual awe. Scripture says, "The heavens declare the glory of God; the skies proclaim the work of his hands" (Psalm 19:1).

More than ever, I see God's handiwork in the colorful pigments of fruits and vegetables chopped for dinner, rainbow hues whishing around the laundry machine, and pale mocha freckles splashed on Tanner's cheeks, and in observing these pint-size details, I connect to a substantial God. Traveling invites an appreciation for cultural wonder when I follow cobalt Spanish tiles enticing me to a Seville café, a regal bridge serving as the backdrop for a lunch of a crunchy, prosciutto-hugged baguette. Chalky cobblestone streets of Portugal contrast with berry punch bougainvilleas draped across vanilla walls. Heaven mirrors Kauai's beryl waters as Bry and I float in sparkly liquid toothpaste.

Even in my dreams, God shines light on colors never before discerned. I'm convinced God woos us as we sleep, with our dreams, with visions. One dream inspired a yearning for heaven, as my senses were wakened even in sleep. A lush field served as the background, with a weathered cream-colored fence reaching for the horizon as far as my eye could see. I remember the air shimmering with almost a rainbow hue, as if caught in a reflection. Heaven set the scene. Out of nowhere, a stunning peacock leaped over the fence and approached me. As he pranced, a thousand diamond light particles caught his feathers, and for a moment, pastel orange dots peppered the eyes of his plumage, and he glowed. As he peered in my direction, I held my breath. Even as I dreamed, I knew this scene was a glimmer of what eternity holds. It was hand-created for me, and I wonder, have you had your own dreams that hint of forever, colors and dimensions too indescribable for words but enough to stir your soul toward GODsense, toward a sharpened longing for more?

What if God allows our waking hours to be painted as vividly as our dreams? What if our favorite faces, the table we set for Taco Tuesday, and the peacock feathers I arrange in everyday bouquets point back to a real Maker?

GODsense.

He takes utter delight in inviting us to feel alive with colors, tastes, goose bumps, sounds, and aromas that offer dimension to the otherwise dreary. What if GODsense is a gift for average hours and real-life circumstances, an engaging way to pull back the earthly curtain and celebrate a foretaste of heaven?

I turned the last page of Dad's legacy journal to read his final thoughts scribbled by inky pen: *I will see you in heaven, but until then. . .enjoy the journey.*

11
DANCING IN THE ROUTINE

An Invitation to Embrace the Ho-hum of the Everyday

Every day you may make progress. Every step may be fruitful. Yet there will stretch out before you an ever-lengthening, ever-ascending, ever-improving path. You know you will never get to the end of the journey. But this, so far from discouraging, only adds to the joy and glory of the climb.

—Winston S. Churchill

*D*ance parties are a regular occurrence at the Pogue Cottage. Whether it's scrambling eggs, smearing peanut butter across cinnamon bread, or Tanner and Ty pulling stools to the counter to stir taco seasoning into sizzling turkey meat, it's guaranteed that music is blasting from my dad's vintage radio perched on the kitchen corner. We breakfast bop and after-school groove, and occasionally I sync my playlist to Janet Jackson and bust out a high school cheerleading dance routine, the boys staring wide-eyed as I force my midthirties body to embrace my former seventeen-year-old limber, leg-kicking self.

Evening dance parties, though. *That's* when our fun is taken to a whole new level. With lights low and dollar-bin glow sticks waving, Ty cranks the volume, and radio station roulette is in full force. Tanner spins the channel, and it's country or rap or Bieber fever. You would die if you could see how Ty gets down with a mad booty shake, even to classical

Bach. Because as Li'l Mom says, "Life is too short to be boring." And when we take average moments like preparing, eating, and cleaning up meals and layer them with songs and swaying, we celebrate the ordinary. *Why celebrate?* For no other reason than it's a random Wednesday evening and we can either wish it toward Friday or choose to make memories out of the average ho-hum of a hump day.

You know what I'm finding is an average amplifier? Time. It's as if the clock glares, looking down his pointy nose, and with every *tick-tock* bellows his threats: *You're behind. You're not there yet. You're not on schedule.* And I'm chasing this heart-pounding time restraint as if my day is supposed to unfold like an epic event, when in fact, it's just a day. A routine, normal one, at that. An invitation to persevere.

Perseverance, a much overlooked and understated character trait, releases the clock's jail cell we hold ourselves captive in. Perseverance intentionally dismisses an agenda centralized around our needs. Perseverance embraces how the day's pieces fall together and, by doing so, transforms us to reach for the volume to turn up the music.

Because that's where we spend ninety percent of our time, right? On our very normal couch, in our average home, eating off everyday dishes, cleaning up after dogs that poop, and creating intentionally safe space where disagreements and laughter and chaos occur. Normal rhythms begging us to see Jesus as real. The everyday is not like a shiny musical, friend, where the best version is highlighted with glitz and lights. It's life, and honoring it is a choice.

Matt and Megs became our first couple friends when we moved to Atascadero. She called on a lazy Sunday afternoon. "Would you want to come for dinner?" Ten years later, even after moving back to Southern California, we consider them family. Recently they bought a fixer-upper, and when Matt is off shift from fighting fires and Megan isn't running crazy long races, along with their son and daughter, they pull up flooring, put up siding, and re-create a rundown space into their dream home. On a summer night, they were sleeping in the living room, their bedroom roof bare to the open sky, when a fluke July storm came and dumped all of God's tears straight into the house.

Matt and Megs woke to standing water filling the closets and soaking the floorboards. Thankfully, they have incredible family and friends who showed up and tarped, wrapped furniture, and drained gallons of water from their master bedroom and hallway. They were now behind on their renovation plans, their house sopped with water-stained damage, but do you know what Megs inspired me with shortly after the fiasco? She said that despite the setback, God met them in the storm and gave them a reason to dance. "We had friends and family calling, texting, helping all night. We never felt alone, not even for a second," she shared.

When the *tick-tock* of an envisioned routine becomes my god, when life ignores my precious memo and steals my dependent focus, when I lose all desire to dance in the average, I take up a critical dance, a complaining waltz. The anxious pounding of my heart drowns out my choosing to see Him in the storm. And if I'm honest, more days bring unexpected drops than perfectly planned mists. My response in the ordinary builds perseverance for the torrential downpours, creating space for deep faith. Only then can I embrace buckets of water falling on bare floorboards and framed walls and crank up the music.

God, I know You are real in unplanned storms, in rain-drenched remodels. You bring people out of the woodwork to lay tarps and pitch tents and make tea. You are reorienting my heart to a new schedule, a holy time frame, and when I cease fighting and release my oh-so-precious minutes to You, perspective is offered and perseverance invited.

Isn't it easy to assume that God mainly grows our spiritual hearts to connect with Him in mountaintop experiences, those camp highs where He speaks loud over bonfires and through life transformation? That worked when I was younger, but I need to know that faith is built in volume, not through events. Through average, grown-up, "showing up and responding to His itinerary before mine" type of days, as I welcome Him to speak into the valleys and hardships and unknowns, not just the peaks. In lesson thirty-five of fifty in her book *Be the Miracle*, Regina Brett acknowledges, "Every experience, no matter how mundane or small, contains a lesson, a gift, a blessing if we take it spiritually, not personally."[29] I'm choosing the spiritual perspective. I did the personal one for far too long.

Josh, one of our church's speaking pastors, offered a poignant sermon on experiencing God in simple ways, when we so often strive for Mount Everest faith. He shared an illustration of how it is impossible for fruit and flowers to grow at the top of a snowcapped peak where oxygen is thin and nutrients nonexistent. Down in the plain soil, the dirt, the manure, the real-life stuff, is where God tills, plants, and repurposes our plans to grow steadfast souls.

So why is it I feel as if grander experiences equate an epic faith? Isn't it, in fact, the other way around? The deeper the dependency, the down-in-the-mess, Jesus-clinging experiences like loss and pain and rejection make for a more robust relationship. The higher the mountain doesn't mean we are closer to God, for it's in the average details of today that we get to put our faith into practice. And when I find myself hoping to trade in for bigger and better, including our house, our lifestyle, our (*ahem*) kiddos, I'm holding tight to where I spend the majority of my time, in the average, where the ordinary is epically best.

The best car is the one I'm driving.
The best job is the one I'm working at.
The best family is the one I have.
The best home is the one we live in.
The best spouse is the one I'm married to.
The best kids are the ones we are raising.
The best wardrobe is the one in my closet.
The best meal is the one before me.
The best talent is the one God gave me.
The best life is the one I am living. Today.

Let's live our lives on purpose, shall we? Be it in flooded floors, playing in the sandbox, or waiting in line at the DMV, count me in, however unplanned detours invite. God meets us in the simplest of moments and transforms our minds to view our schedules, work, parenting, and responsibilities as a way to dance in the storm.

Nothing, my friend, is wasted. God is using every drop—whether from rain or tears or sparkly paper thrown in celebration—to urge us to keep going, keep giving, keep living in today. Keep pushing against the social norms, the false expectations, the racing against the clock to achieve, arrive, and get there. There is no *there*. There is only *here*. As

Liz Gilbert urges in *Big Magic*, "You don't just get to leap from bright moment to bright moment. How you manage yourself between those bright moments, when things aren't going so great, is a measure of how devoted you are,"[30] and I don't want to wait to celebrate how God meets us only in the ginormous occasions but in the simple ones, too.

My friend Tay reminded me of a valuable lesson in honoring the ho-hum when she shared about how her oldest daughter, Thompson, expected for all of life to mirror Disneyland escapades. As Disney season pass holders, their family found themselves at the theme park weekly. Wishing by the castle, enamored by the parade, caught up in the whimsy of a fairy-tale break from the everyday grind of homework and chores and family routines, Disneyland offered a mountain-high distraction.

One day Thompson came home from a friend's birthday party, and at six years old, her hand on her hip, complained to her mom, "It wasn't as fun as Disneyland." Please imagine Tay's face with me.

We are creating a selfish monster, Tay thought. *This girl believes any experience has to live up to a Disneyland-ish expectation.* After a come-to-Jesus powwow with her husband, Tim, they decided to pause their family Disneyland tickets, in hopes of bringing back good old-fashioned family time with imagination and backyard play. Encouraging their kids to entertain themselves for fun, instead of believing they had to be entertained, was their goal.

A few weeks later, Tay passed an open bathroom door and paused when she saw Thompson lip-syncing to *colorful* lyrics. Her daughter was belting into her hairbrush, and her mirrored reflection showed a young girl fully in the moment.

Tay realized she had a choice: she could harp on her daughter for listening to music past her maturity level and shut her dance party down, or she could jump in and celebrate an ordinary "it wasn't long ago I was doing the same thing" moment. I adore how Tay chose to waltz into the bathroom, blasted those lyrics for the whole house to hear, and joined Thompson, as they shared a connecting bond as mother and daughter.

Tay intentionally embraces family pandemonium, even in the middle of house projects, homeschooling, and sibling rivalry. Instead of waiting for monumental events, they commemorate a collection of average hours, which makes for an abundantly imperfect life.

The tension between wanting perfection or wanting to experience "this right here" will always exist. When I lift up a mirror to what today holds, a million choices reflect back. How will I respond? Will it be life-gulping or self-gratifying? Wouldn't you rather dance through the routine than resent, criticize, complain, escape, or abhor it? Isn't it the reality that most of our days *are* spent in the average: working, cooking, cleaning, parenting, coaching, and sometimes just plain surviving?

After talking with Tay, I tucked Tanner into bed, and out of curiosity I asked him, "T, what's your favorite thing we do as a family?" What I thought he'd refer to? Grand adventures like when we went to the zoo, or that one Disneyland visit. Or Legoland. So I was blown away by his response. He didn't bat an eye before his words came: "I like it when we play and have dinner together as a family."

Wow.

At the root of believing that *epicness equals value* is the core fear that my story is not epic and therefore lacks purpose. If I pad my self-worth with grand vacations and life-changing prayer nights and, on the rare occasion, incredible parenting moments, those circmstances will distract from the reality that my story is ever so simple.

Do you ever feel this way? That your story needs to be huge and spotlighty and world changing in order to matter? That somehow God can't use you just as you are, where you are?

Epicness, I'm finding, is an unobtainable expectation, a dream I've created in my head that suffocates sincere joy. When I put down contentment and pick up the lie that *wow* moments hold the most value, I resent reality. Reality, however, brings freedom when I recognize epic is our everyday.

Epic, in my book, is having real conversations with my husband—the kind where we can talk back and forth and compromise.

Epic is sitting with new *and* old friends, honestly sharing our fears and praying God's truth into those areas.

Epic is real life.

It's making our rented cottage an inviting home; it's wearing my husband's high school wrestling sweatshirt, having Taco Tuesday tradition, and taking advantage of beach bike rides.

Epic is driving to Palm Springs for a long weekend and watching our boys learn to skateboard, fall, and get back up.

Epic is when we celebrate anniversaries that respect our bank account.

Epic is a mind-set of making the most of what we have.

Epic is when, as Tanner says, "we play and have dinner together as a family." Tiny repetitions done night after night around a nicked kitchen table, where we ask one another,

"What was new, hard, fun about today?" When I dismiss the way God shows up in the average, I dismiss how much He longs to come alongside the unremarkable minutes making up today. Every tiny fragment matters; it belongs to a bigger story, a larger picture. Today beckons hope. When I plan for an orderly, controlled agenda, He asks, *"What's more important: getting through it or living in it?"*

Epic is celebrating my story. And epic is celebrating your story. And it doesn't depend on the level of grandness or cost but in how content we are with our everyday lives.

Weeks after my dad's death, I dreamed of him. He was sitting inches from my face, his spectacled eyes serious, and I recall the earnest cadence of his words.

"Bekah, I want you to live in today." Then with a sense of sacred urgency, his nose almost touched mine.

"Just *live* in it," he urged. "Live *into* it."

I woke moments later, my heart thumping, and whispered thanks to God for a palpable dream even while the raw ache made me miss my dad more. God used my father's words to woo me toward His presence once again. To live *in* Him. To live *into* today. To enjoy today. To invite me to seek His peace when my inner fan's whir drowns out real time joys because I'm too focused on running off to the next event instead of savoring the moment I'm already in.

Does your average day feel like pushing Play on *Groundhog Day*? Is your "normal" the same thing day after day after day? Do you long for more purpose, more achievements, more affirmation?

When you take repetitive "Does this even make a difference?" perseverant steps and try to love your crabby coworker, or try to connect with your neighbor, or try to love those little kids when you really just want to share an adult conversation, do you find yourself looking at the clock? Do you discover that familiar sense of feeling behind and wondering when the next Disneyland-ish day is coming? It's so easy to miss out on dancing on those days, isn't it? After talking with a friend regarding her *Groundhog Day* situation, this letter poured out. Maybe you can use this gentle reminder, too.

Dear _____,

When you feel frantic about today, frustrated by the ordinariness of your routine, and start to doubt the passions, dreams, and gifts I've placed in you, remember I am near.

And here.

I am not "out there" or "in that job."

I am not "over there" or "hosting that" or "planning that" or "making that money" or "buying that shirt."

I am here.

I am in the mundane details—the cuddles of infants and putting on of shoes. The paying of bills and attending of meetings.

I am in the preparation of meals and in welcoming people into this home. The washing of sheets and being available to answer a heart's cry.

I am in the tears and smiles and songs and squeals. I am in the problems and questions and clarifying work of communication.

I am here.

As you go through the routine, imagine being in the moment with Me. I am in the spit-up and nails in tires and grocery shopping and laundry piles. I am in the couch dates and cookie baking and creative inspirations.

When you are in the "least of these" moments, really, I am with you.

And so, as you wake, when you glance at the clock and count ahead, when you find your mind desperate and living in fast-forward, please take refuge in knowing you are not behind or ahead. I have you exactly where you should be.

With Me.

As the clock ticks and his face glares, know that I am in the feet you are surrounded by, the voices you hear, the hands you hold, and the jobs you do. I'm in those closest who offer a safe embrace.

I am here.

Not "in that" or "over there."

I am creating, preparing, stirring, and growing something beautiful in you.

Contentment cannot be given but must be journeyed.

It is here I will transform the clock's steady hands into moments of peace.

I am here.

I am for you.

I did not bring you to this point to desert or abandon you but to give you life to the fullest.

Trust. Let go. And you will see.

Your Father

After our boys nod off to Neverland, Bry and I love a good movie and bar of chocolate. Food, music, and movies—they taste and sing and stir me to hold today as an anticipated gift. *About Time* is one of my faves, yes, partly because

I heart Rachel McAdams, but mostly for the inspiring message about choosing to live in what today offers. Tim, an awkwardly endearing young Brit, comes from a line of men who can travel back in time. His grandfather uses the time-travel gift to squander money and ends up dying alone. Tim's father time travels to read every book he can cozy himself up with, savoring all of Dickens three times over. Tim's dad encourages him to use his gift for something good, as well. Immediately Tim knows what he'll go back to the past for: love. He wants to find love.

Throughout the movie, I die laughing as he attempts to woo Mary, Rachel McAdams's character. Royally botching it once, twice, thrice, he succeeds the fourth time, introducing himself without making a fool, and eventually wins her heart. Intermittently Tim time travels to talk with his dad over their bond of Ping-Pong, to propose, and to help get his hurting sister out of a destructive relationship. He chooses to journey back in time, always for the sake of love. At the end of the movie, his words have me in tears, for he no longer wishes to journey backward but to fully embrace whatever pain, joy, disappointment, or tension that day holds. He shares, "I try to live every day as if I've deliberately come back to this one day, to enjoy it, as if it was the full final day of my extraordinary, ordinary life."[31] And today, most likely, will overflow with ordinary moments. What it won't hold is another chance to celebrate it, to dance *into* its fabulous averageness, to grab your babes and whisk them around the kitchen, to look into the eyes of a spouse who knows you through and through and whisper, "I'd choose you again. Even when it's hard." To pay bills and scramble eggs and pick up dog poop, knowing today will never come again, and by welcoming what comes is to applaud perseverance.

How do we honor the microscopic details of today? How do we experience God real in the routine? We choose them. Deliberately. With consideration and reverence. Even when I wake at 6:00 a.m. to a typhoon of boys singing at the top of their lungs and shouting, "I'm hungry," a puppy scratching to go outside, wishing I could snag *ten more minutes* in a cozy bed and pause real life, it's *my* typhoon. It's my chosen life. Even with unexpected storms.

At the end of a full, "gave it my best" day, I tiptoe near our sons' bunk beds and kneel to smooch Ty's butter cheeks and hold his dimpled fingers and breathe in his brown sugar scent. I take a picture. An emotional, spiritual, present-encompassing, close-my-eyes-and-remember-this-day picture. And then a physical picture. I do it to grasp this moment permanently, knowing I want to choose it again tomorrow and the next day. Then I hoist myself to Tanner's top level and stroke his curly hair, lay a hand on his strong chest, and *psht* goes my phone.

Savoring the ho-hum of the everyday, even when it feels like tedious work, adds lively steps and beautiful lyrics. A connecting rhythm overlapping with stories, faces, and dance parties missed if not engaged in and enjoyed.

And today? It's quite epic, indeed.

12
TURNING OUTWARD

An Invitation to Serve beyond Ourselves

No one has ever become poor by giving.
　　　　　　　—Anne Frank, *Diary of Anne Frank*

*A*mong pressing conversations I have with the Almighty, the most important, by far, is, "Why, oh why, wasn't I born British?" I mean, I would have been such a fabulous Brit. Their tea. Their accents. Their witty, dry humor. And, of all things good and holy, their *Downton Abbey*, people. Maybe when I enter the pearly gates, the good Lord will make me new in a repurposed, British sort of way.

If you have your wits about you, you, too, are a *Downton* lover. If not, grace abounds, and to Netflix you must go (said in a British accent, of course). In *Downton Abbey*'s season four, there's a moving episode where Isobel Crawley fights depression after losing her son, Matthew, to war. As a philanthropist and people lover at heart, Mrs. Crawley faces grief head-on, and with it, a choice in how to respond to her painful loss. Will she shut herself in and, by doing so, paralyze her soul? Or will she choose to turn her loss outward and use her story for a redemptive purpose? In a decisive swoop, she opens her large estate to host invalid soldiers. She fills rooms and hallways and tables with fresh sheets, medical supplies, and abundant food. In doing so, she doesn't ignore or shove down her grief but finds healing in serving others who are suffering. As the compelling episode unfolds, we notice Isobel soften. We watch her regain her passionate self, but with a stronger, more purposeful dedication and focus.

Giving of ourselves in the wake of grief is perhaps the next closest spiritual act to touching God Himself. We are made bitter or better because of our circumstances. When we make a decision to use our pain by taking the focus off ourselves and placing it with passionate perspective on another, faith is planted deeply in the fertile soil of knowing loss. When this selfless behavior becomes a habit, blooms are plucked from strong branches and given away as bouquets to thankful souls. How can we use the gifts we are given right where we are to be Jesus' hands and feet to those who need care the most?

Turning outward is fueled by our hardest days, when we let go of controlled plans and reach beyond ourselves with a desire to reflect Real. But when the blues invite, isn't it easy to wallow in our stuckness? We map out our lives, knowing how they ought to unfurl, but when details go awry, do we focus on the rearranged aspects or on how God is using the detours to bring our attention to people rather than to our goals? Sometimes we just want to throw the covers over our heads and chalk our blues up to "one of those days," and for those occasions, friend, there's grace. But after a while, if we allow the blues to become our identity, we are stunted, not grown, by hardship. Challenges—however they come—must be journeyed through in order to experience healing, removing the focus from ourselves and putting it on others. As Barbara Brown Taylor beautifully shares in *An Altar in the World*, "The great wisdom traditions of the world all recognize that the main impediment to living a life of meaning is being self-absorbed."[32] When I use my in-the-middle story to come alongside hurting souls, relatability and compassion and the sacred art of giving are born. Navigating hardship is like trudging through deep, sticky mud. Underneath, movement is taking place, but it often feels like millimeter-ish, heavy, slow-motion steps. The truth is, journeying forward is a process—a messy one at that—and when I pull from my own pain story to meet yours, my focus no longer lingers on my affliction but on the opportunity to put tangible meat and potatoes to Jesus' words: "It is more blessed to give than to receive" (Acts 20:35 ESV).

When dim circumstances surround, it's as if the light we carry is stifled within, snuffed out; it only smokes and chokes and clouds clarity, causing further suffering. But when we take our light, even with a shaky hand, and share it with another, we turn our pain inside out; and in doing so, compassion and a spirit of sacrifice are born.

Isn't it easier to hide and wave the independent "I've got this" card even though you crave connection and community? Behind the pain, do you long to put yourself out there, even though it's scary and vulnerable and asks you to leave your cozy dark hiding place?

Turning outward is worth it.

I know this because I'm asked to choose, on a daily basis, whether I'll succumb to my circumstances or turn my feelings outward and be available to how God wants to use my imperfect situation. Some days I stay put in my stinky funk, allowing smoke to swirl and choke any love that God wants to pull out and pass on. On other days I respond to His Spirit's nudge and come alongside someone else who is holding the same concern, and whisper, "God's not going to waste your pain. He's going to use it in beautiful ways. And if you can't see it now, that's okay. I'm here as His mouthpiece to say, 'You are seen. Where you are today is noticed. I'm affirming your process.'" I find those days are lighter and freer and have little to do with me.

When I make a conscious effort to turn outward and let my light flicker brightly, I experience the truth of Charles Dickens's words: "No one is useless in this world who lightens the burdens of another."[33] When I step out of my comfort zone to assure another hurting soul that she is not alone, I am ministering healing in the form of love. Where before I thought serving was essential to feel better, I now understand that it's not about giving with the motive of trying to make my icky feelings go away, but to use my discomfort as a catalyst for compassion. To come alongside and say, "I get it. I'm in the thick of it, too. Let's journey this together for today." What does turning outward look like? It's about honoring the simple steps in our suffering process; it's about setting aside our need to check off a perfectly planned life and instead clinging to the Savior. And as I do, His peace and freedom and bigness overwhelm and propel me to share. I'm finding turning outward starts with responses like these:

- *God, I feel scared right now. Is there someone else who is scared who You can bring to mind so I can offer her a glimpse of how You see her?*
- *God, I feel cranky today. How can I use what I have to take my eyes off myself and plant them on another?*

Turning outward encompasses everything God is about: relationships. Intimate, Father-known, Jesus-dependent,

Spirit-saturated type relationships. Relationships that involve giving and receiving and then giving again, from a space of being known and enough. He gives. We receive. Then we give. Turning outward is like putting on "selfless" glasses. It doesn't change how the situation looks, but it does shift the perspective from me to Him to others.

Love God. Love others.

I'm convinced God meets us, knows us, and offers a dependent relationship in our pain, but He doesn't let us stay there. He uses our suffering to encourage and relate when others need comfort. He doesn't ask us to give so others will make us feel better, but as an invitation to choose to walk alongside a hurting soul. Perhaps compassionate pain is where healing begins.

Suffering attracts sufferers. Like magnets, when Jesus is at the center of your pain, do you find yourself drawn to the knowing arms of others who have survived the process of peeling back raw grief layers? We get it. We are an afflicted crew, you and me. There is something deep and powerful about linking arms and, as an imperfect community, turning ourselves inside out so others can better relate to our messy insides.

In my time of grieving after my dad's passing, I spoke with women, moms, mentors, leaders, and friends who were hurting. Illness. Infertility. Miscarriage. Marriage miscommunication. Family pain. Work challenges. Parenting frustrations. Hard knock days. Throw in friendship and faith dynamics and having to plunge the occasional toilet. We needn't look long or far to find an excuse to cash in the day for the blues card.

But do we really want to stay there? Is that truly abundant, fullness-to-the-brim living?

As I took notice of all this pain in others, I felt stirred to dream. Dreaming gets me in trouble because I'm not able to dream small. Nah, we're talking mountain dreams, friend.

People are hurting—maybe I'll start a conference. Okay. No. *Hmmm. People are lonely and sad and ashamed. Let's start a company and sell upcycled products to show them God is using their story for His glory.* Okay, calm to the down, Bekah. Think. How do I naturally spend time on a weekly basis? How can I use what I'm already passionate about to bring cheer? How can I use my pain of loss and offer compassion to someone's fragile heart? How can I use simple, everyday ingredients to give tangible empathy to a sad soul?

So I started where I was, with a passion for baking, by speaking love in the form of sweets. Out of the oven and into my head sparked the idea: Soul Sweets. The boys and I baked Mana's Chocolate Chip Cookies for friends who welcomed twins, now having four kiddos age four and under. We took a double batch of brownies to our neighbor who recently lost his beloved dog, Sammie. We delivered Oreo cheesecakes and shakes when a friend's hubby lost his job and when another friend's kids were driving her bananas. And we gave for no other reason than it was Thursday and a certain soul needs ever lovin' sweets. On a morning doughnut run, Ty befriended a pair of homeless twins who referred to themselves as (are you ready?) Daryl and Darren, the Double D Brothers. I about died from giddiness at watching our five-year-old sacrifice his sprinkled prize to strangers, his heart expressing selflessness in turning outward.

When I find myself itchy to serve or help, my tendency is to assume that giving must be done in grand gestures instead of with a batch of sweets. But isn't there something about dessert that whispers decadence and a nudge of "extra" to a hurting soul?

The week my dad lay in a coma, my friend Ber called. "What do you need?" she asked. Days before, our Nurture table chose recipes from a dog-eared copy of Shauna Niequist's book *Bread and Wine*, and over a china-plated, full-hearted dinner party, we enjoyed a majority of her staples, and each guest went home with a bag of breakfast cookies to devour come morning.

"I need breakfast cookie ingredients," I told her. "Coconut, bananas, oats, and chocolate chips. . . ," I rattled off, baking suddenly becoming a voracious need. When she showed up at the hospital and walked me outside for fresh air and conversation, her gift of grocery bags soothed my aching soul. Later that evening at Li'l Mom's home, mashing bananas, stirring oats, and pouring chocolate chips brought a therapeutic calm to the unknown. When I heaped mounds of dough into the oven so our family could enjoy breakfast cookies, I felt grounded in a normal sort of, "this is what I do at home" way. Baking soothed the uncertainty of hospital dread. Perhaps God plopped the idea of Soul Sweets into my mind even that day, knowing healing begins when my mind is able to occupy itself with baking and sharing.

My friend Christine lost her brother, 2nd Lt. Mark Jennings Daily, when he was killed by an IED on January 15, 2007, in Mosul, Iraq. He left his wife of eighteen months behind. *Eigh.teen months.* Countless afternoons after Dad died, I sat at the kitchen table from Christine's childhood, crying and angry, processing all the lovely grief feelings that tumble out when someone passes. With gentle knowing, she offered herself, her story, her understanding. As I listened, I noticed the name of her younger brother carved into the soft wood of the table—*Mark*, in scrawling, little-boy print. It's a reminder of his life still present when they sit as a family to enjoy a meal.

Isn't that life? Where we strive for high marks, gold stars, and affirming pats on the back, down days often usher the chirping of crickets and silent, still air.

But all of a sudden, a teacher sees you. He or she affirms a skill you have in singing, arranging numbers, or piling letters together.

A friend seeks you out and gives you encouragement when you most need it.

A boss validates your efforts.

A bunch of marks and dents and dings come with the territory of living, but what if we respond with outward thinking and, on our worst days, walk into a room and see just one soul and give? Give of our encouragement and applause. Give of our time and priorities. Give of our energy and the truth that today is so much more joy filled when we make it less about our self-focused needs and more about God's selfless relationship.

When I literally get out of my comfortable cottage and make myself visible and available on our front lawn, tossing the football or kicking a soccer ball with Tanner and Ty, the neighbor kids stop by to jump off our cement stairstep wall, and relationships begin. Then I'm choosing to turn myself inside out. And if I take it a step further and create cookies or brownies and pile them in our car and deliver cheer in the form of Soul Sweets, that's my contribution. Turning outward, when all I really want to do is stay within, is where true joy is experienced.

At book club, a friend asked each participant, "How do you feel like you are using your light in the dark?" Her question struck me with such simplistic power, because don't we do that every day: choose? How are you using your light in the dark? Where are you choosing to illuminate how God is authentic and present and working? Even in your frustrations, pains, and disappointments? In your grief and "just because" funks? How are you choosing Real?

Living outward is a result of focusing upward. Turning outward starts with prayer, a conversation of listening and doing. Of noting how our faith perspective grows bigger than our agenda when we ask God, "How do You want to use my situation as part of Your massive plan?"

Where do you naturally use your talents and gifts? How can you pour your passion into someone when the hard days come? What brings life from your fingertips? How can you share your joy with another soul?

Em is a phenomenal card maker. Truly. Anytime it's anyone's birthday, it's like, "Em, you got this, right?" And she brushes it off like, *no big deal*. When I sign my name, I'm like, "Really? You just whipped this bad boy out?" And she's rolling her eyes and blaming Pinterest, but I keep telling her, "One day you'll be a famous stationer and Kate Spade will be calling you, and over tea, wanting papery advice." Em's art brings our community joy. She uses the minutes when her daughter rests to create one-of-a-kind cards. In doing so, she takes her mind off the worries of comparison or feeling "not enough"—inward thoughts that could easily snag her if not turned outward.

Talented, uber-inspiring souls who use their stories to give hope compel me. Laurelbox, a company I "met" through

Instagram, offers a tender glimpse into creatives who use their passions to care for the hearts of hurting women.

Laurelbox was started by cousins Johanna, a former museum fund-raiser, and Denise, a design expert with a knack for vintage décor. In 2014 they connected for an annual trip and shared about how they were simultaneously walking alongside friends who had lost babies. Denise scoured the Internet and Etsy looking for the perfect gift "to let my friend know I loved her and her little baby I'd never met." She had a gift made and later asked if it had nourished her friend's soul. The grieving mom admitted it hadn't. Thus began a journey to create gift boxes for women in seasons of difficulty. Johanna and Denise passionately offer tangible gifts to devastated hearts, especially women mourning the loss of an infant, child, parent, or friend. Handmade or teamed with local artisans, their custom Laurelbox can be filled with jewelry, scriptural tea towels (I WILL SUSTAIN YOU being one of my faves), teacups, prints, hand-stamped vintage spoons, and more. When I asked what their company's dream has taught the cousin friends, they shared, "Women offer us the gift of friendship in return. They often ask our advice about what to write on the card, and we are thankful to be voices for those who don't know what to say. When someone orders a gift for a friend, that friend sends it to a different friend. It confirms that Laurelbox nourishes women's souls, and that's the best gift of all." Companies like this are a beautiful reflection of creative entrepreneurs using their heartbeats and experience to speak Jesus' real love to women in difficult seasons.

You may look at Laurelbox and other companies that are turning outward and feel overwhelmed by the grandness of their reach. *What can I do? How can I use my skills to help others?*

you ask. Simple. Start where you are with the gifts you have. Do you feel alive speaking? Painting? Designing? Opening your home and putting out brownies and helping people experience a sense of belonging? Your ministry doesn't have to start big or become monumental; your God-given purpose may start with a prompting of His Spirit and a willingness to be present, to be obedient, to offer joy when you want to sulk. Don't allow others' success to diminish the story God is prompting for your journey. Don't miss out on the gifts He uniquely shines through you. Don't squelch the light He desires to burst forth from you so that others can know Him.

Because God's love, friends, is never self-serving.

How can we start practicing the art of turning outward? We can be available. Text or call a friend who comes to mind. Carry cards in your purse or diaper bag and jot someone a note during a spare minute. Put aside your phone while your little munchers nap or rest and ask God to dream with you, and then write down those basic dreams and ask Him how to go about getting started.

Notice what you're drawn to. What do you naturally do in your spare time? What is life giving and life breathing? God is using your modest passions to share Himself with the world. Do you think He belittles baking or reading or hugging? He's urging your innate zeal to speak genuine affection to people who would otherwise scoff at the mention of a holy God who does bad things to good people.

What if God is using your fervor as means for someone else to find a relationship with the Divine? What if bad days aren't part of our plan but we can use them to point back to Someone who is sovereign? What if we can use uncomfortable situations to teach our children to be aware of others, even when they are afraid or lonely or sad themselves? What if the simple choice in offering our eyes, our ears, and our hands to see, listen, and comfort is not about what we can give but in being changed because we have received from God first?

On couch dates, evenings where I tuck my toes under Bryan and he settles into the pillows, we reminisce about our day. Throughout our married life, we have come to agree that the moments where the most delight is experienced are always, always, always when we focus upward then outward. As Henri Nouwen shares in *Reaching Out*, "When we make ourselves aware of the hospitality we have enjoyed from others and are grateful for the few moments in which we can create some space ourselves, we may become more sensitive to our inner movements and be more able to affirm an open attitude toward our fellow human beings."[34]

When we stop obsessing over ourselves and adapt a selfless perspective, we notice how everyone has pain marks that need to be validated and comforted. Turning outward brings peace to anxious souls and smiles at plans gone haywire. As Nouwen wrote, "We also can become present to others by reaching out to them, not greedy for attention and affection but offering our own selves to help build a community of love,"[35] which brings love full circle. A pivotal part of experiencing the act of turning outward is offering the gift of celebrating someone else, even in our own imperfect circumstances. And that reminds us to continue looking out and beyond and up. Even as He watched His own Son dying, God the Father turned Himself inside out and poured hope, joy, and the promise of peace to us *hunky-dory mates*.

I'm thinking God is totally British.

Cheerio. Onward and outward.

MANA'S CHOCOLATE CHIP COOKIE RECIPE

½ pound (2 sticks) room temperature butter
1 cup dark brown sugar
1¼ cups sugar
2 eggs
1 teaspoon real vanilla
1½ cups whole-wheat flour
1½ cups all-purpose flour
¾ teaspoon baking soda
¾ teaspoon salt
2 cups semisweet chocolate chips
1 cup chopped walnuts (optional)

Blend butter, brown sugar, and sugar until fluffy. Add in eggs one at a time. Then add vanilla. Mix on high for 2 minutes. Sift flours together with baking soda and salt. Add to sugar mixture and mix slowly. Mix chocolate chips (and walnuts) in by hand. Drop on baking sheets by ice cream scoop. Bake at 350 degrees for 15 minutes. For pizookie style, add a generous scoop of vanilla bean ice cream when cookies are fresh out of the oven. Enjoy!

13
YOU MATTER

An Invitation to Shine with God's Unconditional Love

"I have loved you with an everlasting love; I have drawn you with unfailing kindness."
—Jeremiah 31:3

*B*ry was on a three-day work retreat when I decided to give the boys haircuts. Tanner took his normal spot on the back patio bench, holding a squirt bottle while I evened out his curls. Then on to the ears when, *What's that?* I darted closer. *No. Nooo!* My fingers frantically pawed at his temple as I discovered hundreds of tiny, nearly transparent *lice* villains! *Everywhere.* Clinging to his shaggy curls for dear life and no doubt duplicating by the second. So I did what any normal mom whose husband was conveniently out of town lounging by a pool the size of New York City would do. I flipped out! I screamed, *"No! Nooooooooo!"* (I was hyperventilating.) Tanner's eyes were the size of Frisbees, and Ty was jumping on the trampoline fighting imaginary bad guys. I scoured Tanner's hair like a madwoman, squinting, hating those stupid lice. There went our night of making cookies and watching *Wreck-It Ralph.*

My head jerked up and over, and my gaze landed like a tractor beam on our youngest. "Ty!" I was trying to be calm, like, *Hey bud, can you come here so I can weirdly assault your noggin?* but it came out, "Come here! Hurry! Lice have taken over!" Oh. Just wait. It gets better. His brown mop was *cuh-vered*. All over. I watched as the monsters freely jumped, hopscotched, patty-caked on their new brown playground. *Oh my word! Noooo!*

I'd like to claim an insanity defense for this moment. Perhaps I checked out of my body or took a mental pause, because it suddenly hit me. *Hmmm. My head's been itching recently.* And, *aaaaah*, my fingers fly into my desperate-for-a-color mane. I run to the boys' room and press my entire body against their full-length mirror, where the evening sun catches every single tiny lice spawn clutching *my entire scalp.*

Jesus, in the form of Brian and Donna, dear couple friends, swooped in and helped me shower the boys and put them to bed. And, as if them coming to help wasn't enough—*oh yes, she did*—Donna made a party of it and out popped sangria, and I believe candy or sweets were involved. And for the next three hours, they doused my head in grease, and I had one person lice-killing on the right side and another lice-killing on the left, and the three of us were laughing and gabbing and welcoming the wee hours of the next day in a lice-conquering sangria stupor.

I'm convinced our minds work like lice: a single thought suddenly multiplies and takes over. *Where do they even come from?* At 3:00 p.m. I am considering cutting down desserts to every *other* evening, and at 3:01 my mind is itchy with self-deprecating lies triggered by social media, lack of sleep, whatever, and suddenly *I'm the worst mom ever*, and down the black vortex the ugly lies swirl! Given space, the negative murmurs lead only to fearful space unless I acknowledge my unhealthy thought patterns. And sometimes I conquer one negative thought only to greet another.

Licey fear struck again before Christmas.

During the second December after my dad passed, I felt anything but cheery and twinkly. I was Scroogey, to be honest. It was more than one negative thought—or day. The dark month was littered with distracting thoughts, of believing the enemy's lame lies, taunting, *You're too much, too emotion-full. You need to take it down a notch and lessen that passionate soul of yours. You make everyone around you uncomfortable.* The winter days were full of this loud hissing, and I lost sight of God's "making all things new" transformation, lost sight of living out the truth of how God uniquely created me to be me. Instead, I looked for rocks to crawl under, to shrink small and invisible. Combined with take two of Christmas sans Dad/Papa, I weepily wished he were there to sip Chick-fil-A peppermint shakes with us and watch *Christmas Vacation* on repeat. Basically, I was the poster girl for *Living from Fear, Not Love*, and the enemy was cackling at every anxiety-induced thought I internalized.

Isn't that the enemy's ploy? Distract, distract, with a side of distractions. Any way he can manipulate us to forget who we have been created *by* and what we have been created *for*. The lame enemy just wants to turn off the lights.

I wanted Mom *and* Dad decorating Santa's cookies with the boys *together*. I wanted my heart to connect to the knowledge that Jesus' birthday was about to be celebrated. I wanted to live free and confident, to stop analyzing and cowering at every social gathering as if people could x-ray my thoughts and examine the horrible lies I was believing. I wanted my Jesus to shine from within, but paralyzing fear held me in its grip. Somewhere in the midst of "O Holy Night," holiday parties, silver and gold décor, and gifts, it all became too much. So I ditched Christmas Eve service (*yes, you can gasp*). And instead, I cried out for God's comfort. Since I'd grown comfortable with our rhythms, our real conversations, I prayed expectantly, just as Kristi Barefoot, a former women's director at our church taught a group of us at her home. "Ask with confidence and boldness. He is listening, and He wants you to be honest so He can show up. Now pray with expectation." She's a fire lighter, that one.

So I prayed.

"God," I pleaded, "I'm feeling sad and scared and small. I miss my dad. I don't feel like celebrating. So would You please be near? Would You bring a reminder of my dad this Christmas? Would You speak however You want, and could it have something to do with Dad's favorite phrase, 'Enjoy the journey'? Maybe tangibly, like on a ginormous plaque." I was like Gideon asking for a fleece, and I was confident that God, who enjoys giving good gifts to His kids, was eager to answer. "And," I was on a roll now, "could I also get a white barn to upcycle in the middle of Orange County, if that's not too much to ask?" Fine, the last part wasn't an out-loud request. One can dream.

Christmas morning arrived warm and sunny, and as I pulled piping-hot cinnamon rolls from the oven, Tanner and Ty ran down our hall to where the Pogue gift-giving tradition nestled under a modest tree.

Then, after ripping paper, chewing frosted dough, and swigging coffee, we headed down to San Diego to join Bryan's family for Christmas Day. And on the way, I silently prayed, *God please bring a reminder of Dad today, and if it could include the words,* Enjoy the Journey, *that would be super awesome.*

We arrived to coastal-infused Encinitas and, from the porch, were welcomed with cousin laughter, rich coffee cake fragrances, and generous "Merry Christmas" hugs. In a blink, all of us were gathered near the tree, young elves divvying up gifts while the adults breathed it all in—our family, the music, and the buzzing energy—with content smiles. After kids ripped open boxes and squealed in delight, the adults ripped open boxes and screamed even louder (I wonder where they learn this ruckus). Since Bryan is one of four siblings, we've opted for the name-drawing option, an excellent choice instead of buying a billion presents and leaving a swarm of kids homeless for the remainder of the year.

It came my turn, and you won't even believe this. My sister-in-law Kristy had been cahooting (it's a new word) for weeks with Bryan to create a custom-scanned and handmade, silver-encased bookmark with my dad's lifelong phrase "Enjoy the journey" in his own handwriting from his legacy journal. *But wait.* Fingering the pendant-hanging front, my heart lunged and tears streamed as I turned it around and discovered on the back his familiar scrawl scanned from his journal, "I love you so much, Dad." From behind, the tree's lights twinkled.

As I reflect on this moment, my soul beats rush. Isn't God so amazing to use Kristy to answer my heart's cry? I hugged her speechless and wasn't able to communicate until weeks later just how powerfully her gift shined light into the hidden, dark corners of my sadness.

Love flickered bright inside that day. Not only in the physical reminder of God's Spirit showing up through a sister-in-law in unexpected, intentional ways, but in what He spoke to me later.

"I know it's been a hard month," He assured. Then He

posed a question that I wouldn't have otherwise thought of on my own. *"Do you believe you are worthy of unconditional love?"* It took me aback, as my instinctual reaction sputtered, *Oh, of course, silly You. I know I'm loved.* Yet my soul ached otherwise. Fear had already lodged sturdily within me weeks before and now tangled moldy and unapologetically. A safe voice stirred. *"You believe the lie that you are too much, especially when relationships get sticky and love is withheld. I'm here to tell you, that's not unconditional love. I want this year to be one in which you experience unconditional love despite how you respond to yourself or are responded to by people. Okay?"*

It reminded me of what John wrote in 1 John 4:18: "There is no fear in love. But perfect love drives out fear, because fear has to do with punishment. The one who fears is not made perfect in love." Bossy fear. My mind, my thoughts, the way I viewed myself and therefore lived, were cluttered. And that's just not how God intended. Where He dwells, fear is not invited.

Gulp.

Of course the enemy was being a lame-butt (*thanks for the creative word, Ty*). He doesn't want me to be confident and live from the truth that I'm loved no matter what. And he sure doesn't want me to remind you of the same: that the God who created the stunning ocean and stellar universe loves *you* unconditionally. Nope, the ugly deceiver wants all of us to keep going around on the same crazy cycle believing we are weird. Sorry, Satan, you lose.

This was the turning transformation. This was where God plucked the lame-ugly-self-loathing-beat-myself-up-perfectionist tendencies and spun them upside down. He held up a mirror and said, *"Look. I made you on purpose. Everything inside, too, and I am pleased. You are loved. Enough doubting your confidence in whom I made you to be. That shames My handiwork, and I don't make mistakes. Go live in freedom. In your too-much-ness and emotion-full spaces and desire to hug every person you meet. I want you this way. Even if others don't get it, that's okay. You are unconditionally enough. You are much celebrated by Me, and My opinion should matter most."*

Nothing like getting a pep talk from my Father to turn my thought process around and get me to refocus. He continued the love theme with a shower of celebratory lessons. Three, really, that have stuck.

First, He taught me to pay attention when lice-like fears itch by asking His Spirit to nudge my awareness. Our minds are like empty rooms to fill with the thoughts we choose, the very thoughts that create or destroy a safe abode. Here's the catch. Every thought follows a choice: *Do you want truth or lies inside that noggin?* I imagine decorating my mind with focused thoughts designed alongside Philippians 4:8, "Whatever is true, whatever is noble, whatever is right, whatever is pure, whatever is lovely, whatever is admirable—if anything is excellent or praiseworthy—think about such things."

Second, when we seek truth and reach out to community, the enemy doesn't have power over us. Ingrid reminded me of this as I was processing what God was teaching. She stopped me midconvo and declared, "I feel like you just need truth, straight truth right now"—and I reached across the phone and high-fived her wisdom. Yes, it's so simple, but I often forget how truth, God's truth in the form of scripture or wise peeps, sheds light into stale corners. So I went a bit nutso and taped my go-to verses on my bedside lamp—a very cute teal lamp, I might add. Now every morn, before my feet hit the floor, I crane my head left and spot my favorite handwritten verses scribbled on doughnut-bordered paper. Eyes to heart, the truth twinkles with 1 Peter 1:13: "Therefore, preparing your minds for action, and being sober-minded, set your hope fully on the grace that will be brought to you at the revelation of Jesus Christ" (ESV). And penned below, Romans 12:2 reads: "Do not conform to the pattern of this world, but be transformed by the renewing of your mind. Then you will be able to test and approve what God's will is—his good, pleasing and perfect will." I can't tell you how life giving it is to greet the sun focusing my worth on His "steadfast love. . .[that] never ceases; his mercies never come to an end; they are new every morning" (Lamentations 3:22–23 ESV). How great *is* His faithfulness.

My safe peeps are a lifeline. I have asked them to be God's truth reflectors. "I need you," I confessed, "to point me back to truth when I derail and the foggy vortex pulls." At any point, I can text or call those friends and they are there, like shining miraculous stars.

The third way I intentionally celebrate God's unconditional love is by taking responsibility for my thinking. Yes, I realize this isn't a novel concept, but for some reason, when I read *Changes That Heal*, Henry Cloud's words were the first time I ever saw the letters strung together—we "are r-e-s-p-o-n-s-i-b-l-e for our feelings, attitudes, and choices."[36] *Ding!* Yes, we are not victims but permission givers of our thoughts. Remember? We choose which thoughts stay and which lies take a hike. I spend extra time where I'm most reminded of God's unfailing adoration, which usually is in nature, or with people, not in situations where fear readily lurks. By claiming, not questioning God's love, the fullness of life is experienced.

And friend, we can't live fully if we are afraid.

My birthday came on the heels of the start of the new year following my Christmas miracle. To honor a fresh start and still bubbling in all things lovely, I wrote myself a birthday letter. It's a confessional of sorts, but it was also healing, an altar, a declaration that I will no longer fear dark Decembers but will truly celebrate that God loves me unconditionally and wants nothing but greedom (grace and freedom, duh) oozing from my thoughts.

Whether today is your real birthday or, as the Mad Hatter and his crew sing, "A Very Merry Unbirthday to You," this one's for you:

Dear Birthday Girl,

I wish for this to be the year you more fully understand how wide and long and high and deep is Jesus' love for you. And may you believe it deep down in your gut and live from this space. I'll let you sit in that truth for, like, twenty minutes. While eating a mimosa cupcake of course!

I wish for you to know that whether people surround you or you stand alone, you are of great worth.

I pray you will ask people their stories wherever you go and remember that you have a story to tell. May your main characters always be truth and love.

I pray that in the moments you experience the most joy, you will add them to your memory bank and pull them out on hard days.

I wish for you to continue being vulnerable, and when you find yourself getting "in your head," that you will seek truth, text a friend, or start baking, because those things are life giving for you.

I wish for you to laugh at yourself more. Because that means you are risking and possibly failing in the process. But risking nonetheless.

I pray for ridiculously amazing hair days when you're PMS-ing.

I hope when you are tempted to beat yourself up, instead you'll grab a piece of chocolate and say out loud, "I am fearfully and fabulously made."

I wish for you to experience a life worth looking back on.

I wish for you to hear God through a megaphone, notice artistry in hopeless places, and taste life in grateful gulps. I wish for you to seek out people who feel unseen and remind them that they're not.

I wish for you to rest and nap and go lip gloss and shoe shopping for no reason at all. I wish for you to book binge whenever you please.

I wish for you to dance—not crawl—forward. And on the days you crawl, I hope you pour buckets of grace on yourself. Because you are human.

I wish for you to emotionally spoil those boys of yours. And receive their spoiling when they do the same for you.

I wish for you to continue discovering who "your" people are to lean on, ask for prayer, help, wisdom, and dessert recipes. Because you do need them. And they need you.

I wish you champagne cheers and picnic dinners and midweek movies and laughing till you snort.

I wish for you to know when to turn off your brain,

throw the fam in the car, head to the beach, and chase the sun.

I wish you crazy dancing with your hubby and relentless flirting and making out in the kitchen. Dirty dishes can wait.

I wish when self-critical thoughts peck, you will turn outward. Grab a friend her favorite latte and pay her a visit.

I wish for you to pray when you want to complain and give when you want to wallow. And please, be gentle with yourself.

I wish for you to hold nothing back. Gate any doubts and soar.

I wish you bubble baths and belonging and honest conversations.

I pray every "I wish" will become "I'm thankful."

I pray for you to love yourself as much as you love others.

I wish for you to know you are leaving your little mark on this huge world just by being you. And I wish for you to celebrate that today.

Happy Birthday,
Me

After I penned this birthday note, I'm not sure what spark was lit inside me, but as Alicia Keys sings, "This girl is on fire." Where we often plan for simple candles, God shows up with sparklers and confetti.

Fearful souls suddenly came out of hiding—strangers, women, friends, and family—opening up about being afraid of _____ (fill in the lie) and questioning their created purposes. And I was over here doing the happy jig, knowing not *one* horrible thought during the dark December was wasted because now I had the opportunity to encourage them toward celebrating who God made them to be and share truths alongside. I began flaring the *"YOU matter"* mantra like wildfire as I went from *experiencing* God's unconditional love to *spreading* His unconditional love. Because that's what love does; it catches and carries when Jesus is the source.

YOU matter is a daily party God throws, one where He presents glittery party sparklers, supplies the matches, and extends to us the fun task of running and planting them in unexpected hands, only to enjoy watching—once lit, fiery and gold—His love reflected in their glowing smiles.

YOU matter is simply an invitation to celebrate everyone, because when you believe you are loved, you are amped to uplift others who desperately need to be seen and known and encouraged. *YOU matter* is using tangible hands and feet to validate, jump in, and assure the truth of 1 John 4:19: "We love because [Christ] first loved us." That's the Gospel. Plain and simple. In practice, it looks however God's Spirit prompts. For me, it has involved asking, "Who needs celebrating?" only to look around and see friend and foe, homeless and broken, family and stranger, and giddily embrace them in any circumstance or setting with the words *YOU matter*.

Regina Brett is a columnist for the Cleveland *Plain Dealer*, and Li'l Mom literally shoved one of Regina's witty, wisdom-infused books, *God Never Blinks*, into my hands. "You will love this," she said, grinning. Right, she was. Regina shares the story about a drunken man who falls in a hole and cries for help, only to be met by passersby who toss him a Bible or verses or an explanation of why he fell and continue walking by. Then a recovering alcoholic hears the man's cries, jumps in the hole with him, and says, "Don't worry. I've been here before. I know my way out. We climb out together." Regina adds, "The goal isn't to walk around the hole. Or get out quicker. The goal is to fill the hole so no one else falls in it. What do you fill it with? God. Which is to say, love: love of self, love of others, love of God."[37] When I read her words, I knew that I had endured a dark December to jump in the hole with those who go through hard stuff, and as Regina so authentically says, "help others believe that *they* are good enough."[38] That they matter.

YOU matter stirred me to e-mail a person who was heavy on my heart with God's prompt:

> *Teach. Teach your heart out. Teach those kids as though they were your own. You are a blessing to all of them.*

Later I found out that the moment she read the message she was asking God if she was supposed to be teaching.

YOU matter prompted me to check in with writers further along in their journeys to say, "Keep writing. Your voice and perspective matter. I'm with you in this journey." *YOU matter* is championing those who are interested in the same things you are, those who are possibly further ahead or more noticed or more successful, and genuinely telling them, "You are doing a fabulous job. Thank you for letting your light shine. Keep going." You can do this, Liz Gilbert assures in *Big Magic*, "You can support other people in their creative efforts, acknowledging the truth there's plenty of room for everyone."[39] Where fear minimizes, love multiplies.

Saying "You matter" to teachers and coworkers and the homeless man at the park shines God's love from a place of overflow.

YOU matter sends random texts and verses and "I'm thinking of you, that's all" just because someone who needs assurance of God's love sparks to mind.

YOU matter connects a bridge from you, who may have once been captive to fear but have been set free, to others who need to hear the truth. You get to honor Jesus' words found in Matthew 5:47: "If you greet only your own people, what are you doing more than others? Do not even pagans do that?" By extending His hand in the form of yours, looking into someone's eyes, and saying, "I see you. I am for you. And YOU matter," love breathes new life. By offering unconditional love, you are receiving the freeing gift of giving God's love away, trusting His Spirit will show up in even bigger expressions.

Can you imagine? Can you imagine the acceptance and love and freedom you will have if you show even one person each week, each day, that she or he is genuinely valued? When we see—really, truly *see*—people and let them know we're on their team before they even know our name, it changes everything.

I'm convinced that if we become a culture that stops living in fear and instead chooses to believe we are unconditionally loved, this *YOU matter* philosophy has the potential to be life changing.

And it can start today.

With Him.

With us.

Where dark Decembers and distracted lies are replaced with truth and authentic love. With stunningly personal manifestations that exceed our expectations.

Life is no longer a crapshoot where I offer brazen efforts in exchange for a tightly controlled ship. No, today is one I get to live *in* and *from*. To hold my hands open, fully present in response to the vibrant ways God shows up. He joins me to look beyond, up close, and into another's eyes. But first I look within, where He shines unconditionally despite anything I do. In the wise words of C. S. Lewis, "Don't shine so that others can see you. Shine so that through you, others can see Him."[40]

I'm learning to cheer others' wins, to cry with others' losses, to turn grief outward, to embrace the scattered steps He places before me, and instead of saying, "God bless my soul, life is so easy and God is so good," I laugh, and with honesty, utter, "This is so not how I thought faith would look, but God's path proves more spontaneous and life giving, more inner-healing abundant than anything I was creating on my own."

Pass the sparklers, throw confetti, and pray against all future lice visits or anything that threatens your joy. Because this party isn't about taking credit for the details that do stick to our plan, but enjoying the moments that don't. I'm choosing to celebrate each one, the detours, the bumps, the way Jesus transforms from the inside out. As He presents Himself Real, I'm learning to respond with a tenacious welcome, an intimate knowing, and an expectant heart to collect His out-of-the-box pursuits and string them together to resemble one reflective light.

And if you look closely, our gathered glows illuminate His next invitational display: Surprise!

POGUE GIFT-GIVING TRADITION

Something Worn: Dress-up clothes, pajamas, sneakers

Something Read: A book with a handwritten note inside

Something Sung: A soundtrack, musical, or audiobook

Something Experienced: Theater tickets, a sporting event, or a day adventure

Something Played: A board game, sports equipment, puzzles, or interactive games

Something Made: Get creative! Upcycle galvanized rain gutters into shelves or frame piano music to write notes with dry-erase markers.

ENDNOTES

1. Bob Goff, "Bob Goff Quotes," Goodreads.com, accessed December 31, 2014, https://www.goodreads.com/quotes/594710-every-day-god-invites-us-on-the-same-kind-of.

2. Ulrich Henn, "Ulrich Henn Quotes," QuoteHD.com, accessed June 24, 2014, http://www.quotehd.com/quotes/ulrich-henn-quote-all-men-believing-in-god-or-not-are-invited-to-enter.

3. Jeff Shinabarger, *Yes or No: How Your Everyday Decisions Will Forever Shape Your Life* (Colorado Springs: David C Cook, 2014), 168–69.

4. Barbara Brown Taylor, *Leaving Church: A Memoir of Faith* (New York: HarperCollins, 2006), 195.

5. Ibid., 195.

6. Maya Angelou, *Wouldn't Take Nothing for My Journey Now*, "Maya Angelou Quotes," Goodreads.com, accessed March 2, 2014, https://www.goodreads.com/quotes/427696-every-person-needs-to-take-one-day-away-a-day.

7. C. S. Lewis, "C. S. Lewis Quotes," Goodreads.com, accessed October 13, 2014, https://www.goodreads.com/quotes/1180-pain-insists-upon-being-attended-to-god-whispers-to-us.

8. Barbara Brown Taylor, *An Altar in the World: A Geography of Faith* (New York: HarperCollins, 2009), 157.

9. Jerry Sittser, *A Grace Disguised: How the Soul Grows through Loss* (Grand Rapids: Zondervan, 2004), 74.

10. Taylor, *An Altar in the World*, 160.

11. Shinabarger, *Yes or No*, 83–84.

12. Gustav Mahler, "Gustav Mahler Quotes," BrainyQuote. com, accessed July 11, 2014, http://www.brainyquote.com/ quotes/quotes/g/gustavmahl302038.html.

13. Mo Willems, *My New Friend Is So Fun!* (New York: Hyperion Books, 2014), 18, 44, 51–52.

14. Shinabarger, *Yes or No*, 44.

15. Donald Miller, *Scary Close: Dropping the Act and Finding True Intimacy* (Nashville: Nelson Books, 2014), 127.

16. Henri J. M. Nouwen, *Reaching Out: The Three Movements of the Spiritual Life* (New York: Doubleday Dell, 1975), 26.

17. Ibid., 34–35.

18. Brené Brown, *Rising Strong* (New York: Penguin Random House, 2015), 79.

19. Shinabarger, *Yes or No*, 104.

20. Gustav Mahler, "Gustav Mahler Quotes," BrainyQuote. com, accessed February 3, 2014, http://www.brainyquote. com/quotes/authors/g/gustav_mahler.html.

21. Jen Hatmaker, *7: An Experimental Mutiny Against Excess* (Nashville: B&H Books, 2012), 111.

22. Sherry Turkle, "The Psychology of Social Media," Realsimple.com, by Yolanda Wikiel, accessed September 21, 2015, http://www.realsimple.com/work-life/technology/ social-media-psychology.

23. Ibid.

24. Mother Teresa, "Mother Teresa Quotes," BrainyQuote. com, accessed March 2, 2014, http://www.brainyquote.com/ quotes/quotes/m/mothertere158107.html.

25. Ralph Waldo Emerson, "Quotes About Gratitude," Goodreads.com, accessed April 18, 2014, https://www. goodreads.com/quotes/14132.

26. Margaret Feinberg, *The Organic God* (Grand Rapids: Zondervan, 2007), 132.

27. Ibid., 85.

28. Samantha Cortez, "Why Great Brands Appeal to All 5 Senses," *Business Insider*, November 18, 2012, http://www. businessinsider.com/why-great-brands-appeal-to-all-5- senses-2012-11.

29. Regina Brett, *Be the Miracle: 50 Lessons for Making the Impossible Possible* (New York: MJF Books, 2012), 182.

30. Elizabeth Gilbert, *Big Magic: Creative Living Beyond Fear* (New York: Riverhead Books, 2015), 149.

31. *About Time*, written by Richard Curtis, Universal Pictures, June 27, 2013.

32. Taylor, *An Altar in the World*, 91.

33. Charles Dickens, "Charles Dickens Quotes," Goodreads. com, accessed June 25, 2014, https://www.goodreads. com/quotes/18876-no-one-is-useless-in-this-world-who-lightens-the.

34. Nouwen, *Reaching Out*, 79.

35. Ibid. 41–42.

36. Dr. Henry Cloud, *Changes That Heal: How to Understand Your Past to Ensure a Healthier Future* (Grand Rapids: Zondervan, 1992), 162.

37. Regina Brett, *God Never Blinks: 50 Lessons for Life's Little Detours* (New York: MJF Books, 2010), 54–55.

38. Ibid., 55.

39. Gilbert, *Big Magic*, 41.

40. C. S. Lewis, "C. S. Lewis Quotes," Goodreads.com, accessed May 28, 2014, https://www.goodreads.com/quotes/1273084-don-t-shine-so-others-can-see-you-shine-so-that.

ABOUT THE AUTHOR

An everyday Jane, Bekah is passionate about encouraging women to find their identity and freedom in Jesus, to live intentionally, and to celebrate their created selves. As a writer and speaker, Bekah shares about how God is inviting His REAL self to be experienced through life's pits and peaks. She communicates her heart with a relaxed, storytelling style, as if you were sitting on her couch and catching up as old friends. You can find her at the beach, reading, baking, rearranging furniture, or flea-marketing. Bekah and her hubby, Bryan, and their two energetic boys reside at The Pogue Cottage in Huntington Beach, where dance parties are a regular occurrence. Bekah invites you to connect with her at bekahpogue.com.